A DARK
HISTORY
—— OF ——
TEA

A DARK
HISTORY
— OF —
TEA

SEREN CHARRINGTON HOLLINS

PEN & SWORD
HISTORY

AN IMPRINT OF PEN & SWORD BOOKS LTD.
YORKSHIRE – PHILADELPHIA

First published in Great Britain in 2020 by
PEN AND SWORD HISTORY
An imprint of
Pen & Sword Books Ltd
Yorkshire - Philadelphia

Hardback: 978 1 52676 160 6
Paperback: 978 1 52676 681 6

Typeset in Times New Roman 11.5/14 by
Aura Technology and Software Services, India.
Printed and bound in the UK by TJ International Ltd.

Pen & Sword Books Ltd incorporates the Imprints of Pen & Sword Books
Archaeology, Atlas, Aviation, Battleground, Discovery, Family History, History,
Maritime, Military, Naval, Politics, Railways, Select, Transport, True Crime,
Fiction, Frontline Books, Leo Cooper, Praetorian Press, Seaforth Publishing,
Wharncliffe and White Owl.

For a complete list of Pen & Sword titles please contact
PEN & SWORD BOOKS LIMITED
47 Church Street, Barnsley, South Yorkshire, S70 2AS, England
E-mail: enquiries@pen-and-sword.co.uk
Website: www.pen-and-sword.co.uk

Or
PEN AND SWORD BOOKS
1950 Lawrence Rd, Havertown, PA 19083, USA
E-mail: Uspen-and-sword@casematepublishers.com
Website: www.penandswordbooks.com

Contents

Introduction

Tea's proper use is to amuse the idle, and relax the studious, and dilute the full meals of those who cannot use exercise, and will not use abstinence.

Samuel Johnson (1709-84)

Whilst there is infinite pleasure in taking tea, the painted veil of gentility and civilisation that tea wears hides a much darker history.

Today nothing seems more charming and peaceful than drinking tea. Tea enjoyment is seen as one of life's most basic and natural pleasures, but the rise of tea consumption in Europe and Britain is stained with tears and corruption.

Each time we add tea to a pot or lift a cup to sip the revitalising brew we become another link in the fascinating chain of events comprising the dark history that connects our modern tea drinking rituals with ancient China.

In times of trouble and strife or after a laborious day, the desire for a nice cup of tea and a sit down can be overwhelmingly strong. One reason that tea makes us feel good is because it contains caffeine, perking us up and refreshing us while at the same time its healthful polyphenols calm and soothe us. Once considered an exotic herb, tea has undoubtedly infused British lives and history and been the debate of kill or cure health claims.

The history of tea and its introduction to Britain spelled a series of social transformations. The British gradually accepted tea consumption as a sign of refinement and eventually all social classes enjoyed the drink, but as tea flourished and an image of tea as genteel and polite emerged, the concept of a 'proper cup of tea' touted by the advertisers hid a far from unblemished record.

Indeed, the dark underside of tea is a tale of death, drug addiction, exploitation, monopolies, wars and ethnic displacement. While tea became the Western world's favourite beverage it instigated revolution and two wars.

Death by tea was a very real possibility and you'd be lucky if your tea was only adulterated with cherry leaves, acting as a rather unwanted, strong laxative. As fears escalated about tea being the trigger for hysteria and insomnia, the real issue was it carrying the risk of being toxic through widespread adulteration. Unscrupulous businessmen in the Chinese city of Guangzhou (Canton) and England resorted to all kinds of unseemly practices to pad out consignments of green tea. In 1766 an earlier Act of Parliament levying a fine on adulterators was made more stringent by the threat of imprisonment. However, with so much profit to be made from adulteration, the threat of incarceration was not an effective deterrent. Dishonest dealers continued to swindle tea-lovers by adding iron filings and the leaves of other plants, such as hawthorn, and even dying leaves with verdigris, Prussian blue, Dutch pink, ferrous sulphate, copper carbonate and sheep's dung.

The history of tea in Britain does not start with a royal marriage between Catherine of Braganza, daughter of Portugal's King John IV, and Charles II. The story of Catherine making tea popular in England with her refined palate and charming tea etiquette is a pleasant distraction from the true story; one that is tainted with appropriation, pillaging, slave trading, a government-backed narcotics operation, murder and criminal calamity.

We may consider that the aim of taking tea is to share goodwill; we drink tea socially, with friends and colleagues, while important business can also be signed and sealed over a cup of tea. Tea is an important part of our modern-day lives, providing refreshment, revitalisation and allowing time for peace and reflection, but every time we sip from that cup of tea we may consider that our cup of pleasure was once an accursed cup, full of peril. Indeed, the story of this brew is a fascinating and corrupt storm in a teacup.

Storm in a teacup - The term 'storm in a teacup' refers to a big fuss about nothing, but the arguments and fiascos over tea throughout the course of its history have always been seen as very worthwhile and justified.

Chapter 1

The Origins of Tea

Tea is undoubtedly one of the world's best-loved drinks: a staple of millions of kitchen cupboards around the globe, and billions of cups of it are enjoyed every day. Today it is considered a respectable drink that is suitable for polite company, but if you deem tea to be all about floral tea dresses and chintz china cups then think again because tea is a drink with a murky history. Just as good and evil are forever intertwined, so we must similarly consider tea and opium.

The origin of tea is shrouded in myths and stories, so much so that it is difficult to establish its true history from the rich tapestry of mythology. From Chinese emperors to Portuguese princesses, the history of tea is as rich and varied as its tasting notes.

It is true to say that tea is one of the planet's oldest traditions and consequently we have few historic records to indicate where it originated. The earliest writing on Chinese tea is a preparation guide written sometime between 760-762 in the Tang dynasty called *The Classic of Tea*. This account of the growing, manufacture, brewing and enjoying of tea was thought to be the earliest record, until tea remains were unearthed in an emperor's tomb from the Han dynasty, predating *The Classic of Tea* by at least 500 years.

Since myths and legends surround the origin of tea, it is perhaps unsurprising that much of the history relating to its discovery hinges on a mythic Emperor God: Shennong. The celebrated Emperor Shennong ruled sometime before the first recorded dynasty, the Xia, a dynasty that predates the earliest known Chinese writing system. As such there is no archeological evidence to support its existence. Traditional Chinese history credits Shennong as being the first to recognise the benefits of tea as part of Chinese medicine, and it is at this point where history and mythology become inextricably entangled. There are two popular

Shennong, the "Farmer God", tasting herbs to discover their qualities.

versions of the story of how Shennong discovered tea, the first of which involves the mortal emperor calling for a servant to prepare a drink of boiled water. As the servant carries out his duties, a leaf falls from a tree and steeps in the boiling water, unnoticed. Shennong drinks the tea-leaf infused water and is invigorated by its refreshing qualities.

The second version of the story features an immortal god with transparent skin, through which he can directly observe the effect the herbs and plants he eats have on his body. One day, after eating seventy-two herbs (some of which were toxic), he tries tea for the first time and it clears the toxins from his body. A version of this story centering upon a mortal emperor also exists, whereby Shennong – who is reputed to have established a stable agricultural society in China and to have catalogued over 365 species of medicinal plants that became the basis of later herbal studies – was taken ill while on a botanical foraging expedition.

The story goes that while looking for new medicinal plants to catalogue, Shennong was taken by a bout of biliousness and decided to rest under the shade of a tree and hydrate himself. He boiled some water, as was customary, and a few leaves fell from the tree above into the boiling pot. The resulting infusion had an appetising aroma and, on drinking it, he found it slightly bitter but richly flavoured. After drinking it, Shennong immediately felt restored and revived and thus the medicinal effects of tea were discovered.

An alternative story claims that the Indian prince, Bodhidharma, a Buddhist convert who went to China to spread Buddhist teachings during the sixth century, used tea as a stimulant to prevent him from falling asleep during his seven-year contemplation of Buddah. The story tells that Bodhidharma believed that it was necessary to remain awake for prolonged periods in order to meditate and pray. In order to stay alert and awake he chewed leaves from the tea shrub, which acted as a stimulant and sleep suppressant. He thus became the first person to discover that tea can combat drowsiness. An alternative and more macabre version of this story tells of Bodhidharma accidentally falling asleep, and upon waking being so full of self-loathing at his weakness that he cut off his own eyelids in disgust, throwing away the eyelids from which sprouted the first tea bush.

Even setting aside myth and separating fable from fact, the origins of tea still prove difficult to navigate and part of the problem stems from the fact that the Chinese character *t'u* is used in early sources to describe infusions made from several different plants, not just infusions made from tea. By the third century CE, though, a new character, *ch'a*, was developed to refer specifically to tea. *Ch'a* is very similar in its calligraphy to *t'u*, and its development suggests that tea had become such a popular drink that it warranted being given its own character. The word *ch'a* is now sometimes used in English to refer to China tea.

Tea was certainly known as a beverage in the time of Confucius (c.551-479 BCE) and grew in popularity during the Han Dynasty (206 BCE-220 CE). It's worth noting that tea as a beverage during this time would not be something today's tea connoisseurs would appreciate as it would undoubtedly have been a bitter drink due to its raw state. The processing methods of drying and fermenting were only being developed c.650.

By the time of the Tang Dynasty (618-906) tea was the national drink of China, spreading from court circles to become popular throughout

Representation of Bodhidharma.

Chinese society. As demand for tea became greater and outstripped supply, Chinese farmers chopped down increasing numbers of mature trees and stripped the branches of their increasingly valuable leaves. As demand kept increasing so did the destruction of natural tea groves, but thankfully an early ecological disaster was narrowly avoided as order in cultivation and harvesting was introduced and tea planting and growing spread from Szechwan province through the south-west and into Central China. At this time the tea groves of Hunan and Hupei were harvested solely for the emperor's consumption.

Today we are used to seeing tea leaves either loose or more commonly contained within a bag, but in the interior part of China people compressed their tea into bricks and used it as currency to barter. While we are a society that pays for the majority of our services and goods with coins, notes or electronic money, it has taken a while for this system to develop and take hold and primitive methods of payment included teeth, minerals and, in China, tea.

Tea bricks were used as a means of payment from the ninth to the twentieth century in China, Mongolia, Siberia, Tibet, Turkmenistan and Russia. The Chinese emperor himself had the monopoly on the production of tea as the means of payment. The bricks were mainly produced in Sichuan, a Chinese province, but also in Russia. The valuable tea was compressed into bricks for easy storage and transportation was by horse or camel. Tea bricks are not made simply by the compression of leaves but through a skilled process that involves several stages. Firstly, the tea leaves are dried in the sun, then they are removed from their stem and sifted and separated. After separation the processed leaves are placed in a bag and steamed and fermented. The resulting mixture is then cast in a mould where it is then frequently moistened with rice water to bind it and prevent the formation of air bubbles. This would be the process employed for the finest quality tea cakes and would result in a dark brown cake containing just fermented tea leaves. Poor quality cakes, however, could be adulterated with anything from twigs, wood shavings and soot. The adulteration of cakes of varying qualities was rife. In order to bind the tea bricks and keep them solid they would have a variety of substances added, including bovine blood, animal dung and flour. Before being used, the brick would also be put through fire.

All tea bricks were decorated with the individual marks of regions or makers and to prepare the tea, part of the brick was ground down,

Chinese pressed tea block design. In ancient China, compressed teas were usually made with thoroughly dried and ground tea leaves that were pressed into various moulds to create distinctive designs.

and the result was boiled in water. Later, powdered tea was developed from green tea leaves and this gained popularity during the Sung Dynasty (960-1279). Boiled water was poured onto the powder and left to brew, and the resulting tea tincture was whisked into a frothy brew. It was during this period that tea drinking became popular in Japan, reintroduced there by a Zen Buddhist monk who had been studying in China. So, in Japan, it was the Sung method of preparing tea that took hold.

Today, tea bricks are an uncommon sight, with the exception of the post-fermented teas such as Pu-erh, which are still found in brick format. There was a time prior to the Russian invasion of Tibet, before the Second World War, that in preparation for the conquest, the invaders bought up all of the available tea bricks, thus symbolising the importance of tea. Indeed, they felt that by controlling the tea supply, they would be able to control the people who relied heavily on it. A common theme of tea as a valuable commodity, as well as its adulteration, flows throughout history.

A great turning point in the fortunes of tea as a mark of cultural significance was a fascinating account of tea and its benefits written by a Chinese scholar called Lu Yu. By the time he wrote the *Ch'a Ching*, known as *The Classic Tea*, tea drinking was already a fairly common practice in China and was already becoming a refined activity that was little to do with hydration and was instead imbued with artistic, religious and cultural notes. Indeed, a government-imposed tea tax evidences

Most tea bricks ('Zhuan Cha') are from Southern Yunnan in China, and parts of Sichuan Province.

the beverage's growing popularity, and it was at this time that tea was recognised as China's national drink. In this respect, Lu Yu's work did little to promote its consumption or increase popularity. However, *Ch'a Ching* was the single most influential aspect in developing the cultural significance of tea.

It is said that nothing in fashion is ever new and the recent food fashion of mindful eating is certainly not a new concept. Lu Yu wrote in *Ch'a Ching* of the need to slow down when making and drinking tea, and of the importance of paying strict attention to each step and the implement used, ensuring that the entire tea infusing process was undertaken with care, beauty and grace. It elevates the preparation and drinking of tea to a ceremonial status, with a set ritual, and there are guidelines on the appropriate state of mind for the tea drinker, and the atmosphere in which tea should be drunk.

Lu Yu's exacting instructions for the taking of tea are far from our traditional builder's brew. The *Ch'a Ching* begins with an explanation of the tea shrub and how it grows, along with instructions on the correct way to manufacture tea and what weather conditions are to be considered prime for picking. It then goes on to describe the twenty-four implements needed for the preparation of tea. These range from the brazier and the cauldron for heating the water to the roller needed to grind the solid bricks of tea; from the bowls in which the tea was served, to the container for carrying it all. Lu Yu gives advice on every aspect of these implements. Indeed, the right equipment was deemed so important that the author advises that if even one implement is missing it is usually best to dispense with the tea altogether. Tea was not a beverage but a social experience, full of ceremony and etiquette.

Lu Yu then gives advice on where to find the best sources of water for making tea (mountain water from slow-flowing streams), the stages of boiling in order to create the best taste, and also instructions on how to enjoy tea as a sensory experience beyond taste. It is no surprise that it is advised that tea must be sipped slowly and savoured.

To write a book dedicated to the precise preparation and handling of tea in order to capture the unhurried essence of this famed beverage seems on the surface a most reputable pursuit. Indeed, the emphasis upon the ritualised details of tea, from cultivation to brewing and drinking, appear to be purely spiritual. But even in the great teachings of best practices for ensuring simplicity and harmony through tea ceremony, there is a commercial twist. There are stories about how Lu Yu lived for a time in seclusion in the Chekiang Province and came to write the *Ch'a Ching* after a period of deep contemplation; whilst walking in the wilderness, he broke down in tears and was forced to return home, where he had some tea. After feeling revitalised by the restorative properties of the tea he was inspired to write the *Ch'a Ching*. However, a more likely story is that, in the true commercial spirit of tea, the book was commissioned by a group of merchants wanting to extol the merits of tea and popularise the drink that was the basis of their livelihood. Indeed, it could be considered one of the most successful advertising campaigns in history, laying the foundations for what was to become one of the most lucrative and attractive European retail enterprises.

As well as documenting the best practices in tea growth and consumption, Lu Yu also opposes the common practices of adulterating tea and lists some of the things added to it by his contemporaries, including ginger, orange peel and peppermint, as well as other spices. He deeply disapproved of popular methods of tea brewing that called for the additions of flavourings, 'not unlike the swill of drains and ditches'. He advises that the only additions necessary or appropriate to tea are salt, which is added after brewing, and that in the case of 'children who are frightened and tumble without apparent cause', small onion roots be added to bitter tea.

Upon careful reading, Lu Yu's writing hints at a deep frustration that tea was not better understood by his contemporaries. With every single earnest and detailed description of tea production and brewing, Lu Yu's passion for the drink is undeniable and his tea ceremony could put any modern rituals to shame.

The stringent rules of Lu Yu's tea making seem at odds with the modern Western notion of a quick cuppa, which, in many instances, involves throwing a teabag into a cup and pouring over hot water. Despite the rise of coffee drinking, it seems that our modern-day thirst for tea is not in decline, but changing, with our appetite for mass-produced, low-quality products weakening while our taste for premium tea is on the rise.

Lu Yu was concerned that tea should be made in an atmosphere of tranquility and the drinking of it should create still greater tranquility. In modern Britain, most tea drinkers would agree that sitting down with a cup of tea is one of the cornerstones of our society. The familiar act of making tea has long been considered calming during times of stress and trauma and a cup of tea itself has long been thought to enhance that

Statue of tea master Lu Yu in Pinglin.

feeling of peace. While today the accoutrements of tea tend to be fewer and simpler, and there are few of us who have to draw our water from mountain streams, a nice cup of tea and a sit down is still considered one of life's simple pleasures.

Lu Yu's book was certainly influential in his homeland of China, but it was most avidly read in Japan, which looked to China for many cultural inspirations. Tea was no exception and so Lu Yu's teachings served to form the basis for the development of the formal Japanese Tea Ceremony known as *Cha-no-yu*, a ritual that has raised the preparation and drinking of tea to an art form that still flourishes today.

It's hard to believe now, but tea in China eventually fell out of favour as a beverage during the years of the Mongol Yuan Dynasty (1280-1368), as the Mongol rulers considered the drinking of tea a symbol of decadence. However, tea returned to popularity under the native Chinese Ming Dynasty (1368-1644). After years of foreign rule, this dynasty saw a revival of all things considered quintessentially Chinese, of which tea was at the forefront.

It was in this period that tea began to be brewed in a manner more familiar to us today: by the steeping of cured loose leaves in boiling water.

At the same time as the Chinese Ming Dynasty tea revival took hold, tea was first being sampled by Europeans. This is why the method of steeping cured leaves in boiling water to make tea became the tried and tested method used in the West, and remains the most popular brewing technique today.

Up until the Ming Dynasty tea was generally green, but during the Ming Dynasty there was a period of experimentation with different varieties, including fermented black teas, unfermented green teas, and the semi-fermented variety, now known as oolong, which is prized today for its health benefits and complex taste.

It wasn't just the variety of teas that was expanding during this time, but tea's cultural significance. Tea was shifting from being a beverage to becoming ubiquitous throughout popular culture and dominant in literature and art. It quickly assumed an importance in daily life and an iconic status previously reserved only for religious conviction.

Tea was established in Japan by 800 CE, but it was first used for medicinal purposes and it was only much later that the preparation became a ritual of elegance and leisure. The tea plant was supposedly introduced by Buddhist priests returning from study in China and for some years the practice of tea drinking remained the preserve of the priests. They brought seeds, which they propagated, and in 815 the Emperor Saga decreed that tea be widely cultivated and paid to the court as tribute.

Different fermentations of tea. From left to right; green tea (bancha from Japan), yellow tea (kekecha from China), oolong tea (kwai flower from China) and black tea (Assam from India).

For 200 years, tea formed a royal tradition until civil wars took hold between the tenth and twelfth centuries and it suffered neglect. The traditions were far from forgotten, however. The religious community preserved the practices and recipes of many herbal traditions, including tea, but two centuries of war meant that tea and its ceremonies were shelved.

In 1211 the Japanese Zen priest, Yeisai, published his work on tea entitled *Kitcha-Yojoki* which promoted the health benefits of tea. Yeisai had preserved the skills of tea production and preparation throughout the war years, and with peace restored he reintroduced the tea plant to Japan, distributing it throughout the monasteries. He wrote not only of the curative virtues of tea, but also the methods of harvesting and production. Yesai believed that the Japanese nation were sickly due to their lack of tea drinking, proclaiming that tea was a 'divine remedy and a supreme gift of heaven'.

When the Shogun warlord, Sanetomo, became afflicted by severe indigestion, he summoned Yeisai to offer prayers. The Buddhist abbot supplemented his prayers with tea, and after his swift recovery the warlord became a devotee and the appeal of tea soared as a result.

Despite wandering monks promoting tea as they preached Zen during the thirteenth century, by the fourteenth century tea culture had degenerated from the serene and tranquil teachings of Zen into boisterous affairs that could include gambling and the consumption of alcohol. The calm and dignified atmosphere of the Kyoto tea rooms was destroyed by the 'tea tournaments' that saw the ranks of the idle rich bawdily degrade tea to nothing more than a gambling opportunity. The contestants would place extravagant wagers on their ability to identify up to a hundred different varieties of tea. The simplicity and harmony promoted by the Zen monks was eroded and replaced with raucous and vulgar behaviour. Even the government was concerned about the degradation of popular tea culture and attempted, unsuccessfully, to stamp out the practice of tea tournaments. The tournaments survived until the fifteenth century when the Zen movement introduced the *Chanoyu* tea ceremony. These gradually became more and more refined and were synonymous with the appreciation of Chinese art and crafts in a serene atmosphere.

Much of the credit for the resurrection of tea standards and renewed popularity of tea must be given to the work and influences of three Tea Masters. The last of these, Sen no Rikyu (1522-1591), was a key figure in the development of the tea ceremony. Sen no Rikyu was a Buddhist monk with an extensive knowledge in the practices of the tea ceremony, and a close advisor to the emperor. He incorporated principles from the philosophy called *wabi-sabi* – the idea that there is beauty in imperfection and impermanence – into the tea ceremony. He still has followers to this day, perhaps because his teachings are that of acceptance and simplicity, which are of great value in our hectic, modern lives. *Wabi-sabi* is derived from the principles of Zen Buddhism and Sen no Rikyu was the first person to apply its principles to the tea ceremony, giving birth to *wabi-cha* (*cha* meaning 'tea' in Japanese). The introduction of *wabi-cha* led to the simplification of the complex tea ceremony, stripping it down to a bare minimum in order to focus the meaning of the ceremony on the relationship between host and guests. Rikyu dispensed with the pomp and ceremony in tea ritual and even introduced raku pottery, a form of very crude Japanese pottery that he used for his tea ceremonies.

Sen no Rikyu - a portrait by Tōhaku Hasegawa.
(長谷川等伯)

Rikyu himself became the personal Tea Master of the powerful political leader, Toyotomi Hideyoshi, and was his chief aide. Toyotomi Hideyoshi greatly supported Rikyu in spreading the ways of tea as a means of solidifying his own political power – tea and politics were deeply intertwined at this time – but Hideyoshi became increasingly at odds with the rustic and simple aesthetics promoted by his Tea Master. He increasingly viewed Rikyu's methods as a threat to securing his own power and position, and cracks began to appear in their once close relationship. In 1590 one of the leading disciples of Rikyu, Yamanoue Soji, was sentenced to having his ears and nose cut off and being decapitated on the orders of the regent. As the relationship between the Rikyu and Hideyoshi broke down altogether, so came the demise of the great Tea Master and another name was assigned to the dark history of tea. Sen no Rikyu's life ended tragically when, at the request of Hideyoshi, he committed ritual suicide (*seppuku*), which was considered a more honourable death than being executed. The exact reasons behind the suicide are still a mystery.

Despite the tragic departure of Japan's greatest Tea Master, his sons and grandsons continued to practice the 'Way of Tea'. Today the *Urasenke* tea tradition is headed by grandmaster Zabosai Sen Soshitsu XVI, the sixteenth generation of direct descendants of Riyku to hold this position.

Tea is taken throughout Japan by people from all walks of life, and tea ceremonies remain a very social activity, one in which participation by the guests is crucial. There is still an emphasis on harmony, respect, purity and calm, and within the confines of the tea ceremonies formality is the belief that rigidity and structure can, in some senses, be liberating and meditative. The concept that freedom, fluidity and beauty can be found within a strict form is a concept in opposition to the contemporary Western notion that formalism can only restrict art and flow.

Whatever the truth behind the discovery of tea as a beverage, it is certain that it was from China that tea began its rise to global fame as the world's most revered hot drink. However, as tea began to rise in popularity in Europe, so too was its dark side set to take hold.

Chapter 2

The Rise of Tea in
Europe and England

Today tea seems to have established itself permanently as the ordinary, everyday beverage of mankind. We take it for granted that this is the natural order of things. It is often the first thing we reach for in a morning and it is the drink we turn to throughout our daily lives. Tea is often considered a great British tradition and as such very few stop to consider it strange how an Oriental infusion has conquered the world, impacting the relatively recent history of the West.

The tea leaf has enchanted us unlike any other. This 'leaf gold' would soon come to dominate household spending and occupy a place

A traditional English Afternoon Tea.

in the homes and workplaces of the wealthy and poor alike. In 1956, James Laver wrote, in *Twinings Two Hundred and Fifty Years of Tea and Coffee*, 'In spite of the recent vogue for Espresso cafés, the English on the whole, have plumped for tea. They start the day with it, they drink it, very often, in the middle of the morning, they brew it up, in the most unlikely places, from the deserts of Libya to the steaming jungles of Burma. In the north of England they serve it with cockles and even with cold tripe. To be able to make tea is almost a guarantee of being a native of these islands instead of a recent importation.'

Many products and wares from China were known and employed in Europe in much earlier times, but no mention of tea appears in literature prior to 1559. Indeed, tea was first mentioned in European sources in 1559 as *Chai Catai*, 'Tea of China', in *Navigationi e Viaggi (Voyages and Travels)* by Giambattista Ramusio. Ramusio was a revered Venetian author who published a valuable collection of narratives of voyages and discoveries in ancient and modern times.

Ramusio was in a privileged position as Secretary to the Venetian Council. He was able to collect some rare commercial information and to meet many famous travellers, including Hajji Mahommed, or Chaggi Memet, the Persian merchant credited with having brought the first knowledge of tea to Europe. The paragraph containing the early European tea reference reads:

> The name of the narrator was Hajji Mahommed. He told me that all over Cathay they made use of another plant or rather of its leaves. This is called by those people Chai Catai and grows in the district of Cathay which is called Cacian-fu [Szechwan]. This is commonly used and much esteemed over all those countries. They take of that herb, whether dry or fresh, and boil it well in water. One or two cups of this decoction taken on an empty stomach remove fever, headache, stomach-ache, pain in the side or in the joints, and it should be taken as hot as you can bear it. He said, besides, that it was good for no end of other ailments which he could not remember, but gout was one of them.

Although the Portuguese explorer Vasco de Gama opened a trade route from the Orient around the Cape of Good Hope in 1497 it was not until the seventeenth century that tea was imported to Europe. It seems that little happened until the interactions between China and Portugal were well established; the Portuguese did little to advance the introduction of tea into Europe at this time. Indeed, it was not until the Dutch established themselves at Bantam that the knowledge of tea drinking was gleaned and the knowledge transferred to Europe.

In 1678 the Dutch physician and botanist, William Ten Rhijne, who was stationed at a Dutch East India Company trading post in Japan, described, and exported, the first specimens of tea plant to the West. Just months after his arrival in Nagasaki he sent a paper on the tea plant along with tea flowers and leaves. Engelbert Kaempher, a noted scientist and physician to the Dutch East India Company in Japan between 1683 and 1693, was also extremely effective in spreading his understanding of tea to the West. Word of this amazing cure-all plant was further spread by missionaries and diplomats who visited China and described its healing qualities.

Records indicate that tea first arrived in Amsterdam in 1610. It arrived in France in the 1630s and did not appear in England until 1657 when it was first sold at the Sultaness Head in the Royal Exchange in 1658. An early tea advertisement in *The Gazette* No 432, from September 9 1658, reads: 'That Excellent, and by all physitians approved, China Drink, called by the Chineans, Tcha, by other Nations Tay, alias Tee, is sold at the Sultaness-head, a Cophee-house, in Sweetings Rents by the Royal Exchange, London.'

The proprietor of the Sultaness Head was Thomas Garraway and though he was the first person to offer brewed tea to the public, you can cast aside any thoughts of him in a brown coat or apron. Garraway was an astute businessman, a guildsman, and a successful entrepreneur. He was not merely a coffee-house keeper, and the Sultaness Head was not merely a coffee-house. It was a hub for meetings and a centre for commercial and financial negotiations and the striking of deals, in close proximity to the Royal Exchange and the goldsmith banks. The story of Garraway and the Sultaness Head is a complex and interesting one that is intrinsic to that of tea. Spanning the turbulent periods of the Interregnum and the Restoration, Thomas Garraway and the Sultaness Head appeared and prospered in a time of astonishing twists of fortune and extraordinary calamity.

Outside of the habituated few, tea had generally remained little known until the brewed leaf was first served to the public by Garraway.

In mid-seventeenth-century England there was nothing comparable to tea. It was classed as an exotic drug; a distinctive and efficacious Chinese herb prescribed by doctors and purchased from the apothecary, and as such it was a rare and expensive commodity. Sea merchants and sailors returning to England from the East Indies brought tea to pharmacies and physicians, charging exorbitant amounts for small quantities. Men who acquired a taste for tea during their time abroad brought home personal supplies of the leaf, and would seek to enlighten family and friends to the delights of the novel but costly brew.

Tea was a prized commodity and when it first arrived in England it was sold at exorbitant rates to wealthy individuals who locked it away in small decorative tea chests, in order to protect it from sticky-fingered servants. The choice of teas was limited to green tea – for those who could afford it – which could only be used once as its fragrance disappeared, or the cheaper Bohea tea, a black tea that could withstand being brewed more than once. Whatever grade of tea was purchased it was a beverage only to be enjoyed by the wealthy due to the cost. In 1660 Thomas Garraway sold tea in the leaf form at 15s to 50s per lb. It is not surprising that, with tea being so valuable, an Act of Parliament in 1660 levied a duty of eight pence on every gallon of tea made for sale.

It is certain that Thomas Garraway's promotion of tea through newspaper advertisements did much to spread the word of the virtues of the exotic new beverage and the Sultaness Head was further promoted by virtue of its trade tokens: small coins of copper worth a halfpenny and cast or stamped with inscriptions and images on both sides. Two tokens bought a penny's worth of coffee. At a time when small coins were scarce, tokens were used by merchants as change and were redeemable at the place of purchase. The tokens issued by the Sultaness Head bore a female head on the obverse

An illustration of a Sultaness head token.

and an armorial shield on the reverse; the inscriptions encircling the motifs read 'The Sultaness, A Coffee House', and 'Cornhill in Sweetings Rents' respectively. Trade tokens bearing the names of various tea and coffee merchants grew alongside the popularity of these exotic infusions and became a common sight in the eighteenth century.

Garraway saw the potential that tea offered and wanted to persuade customers to embrace this, the new beverage. His 1660 broadsheet, *An Extract Description of the Growth, Quality and Vertues of the Leaf Tea,* was the first detailed document that attempted to encourage new sales and converts. Amongst its claims, 'The drink is declared most wholesome, preserving in perfect health until, extreme old age.' It took time for tea consumption to grow, and despite the best efforts of advocates, tea in England remained an expensive curiosity, as an extract from Ellis's *Letters of English History, Vol. IV* illustrates:

> Letter CCCXI. Mr. Henry Saville to his uncle Secretary Coventry.
>
> Paris. Aug. 12, 1678
>
> These I hope are the charms that have prevailed with me to remember (that is to trouble you) you oftener than I am apt to do with other friends, whose buttery-hatch is not so open, and who call for TEA instead of Pipes and Bottles after dinner, a base unworthy Indian practice, and which I must ever admire your Christian family for not admitting. The truth is, all nations are grown so wicked as to have some of these filthy customs.

As the availability of tea spread throughout Europe the debate over its virtues and possible dangers raged. In Holland, physicians such as Johannes van Helmont recommended it as being restorative against the loss of bodily fluids caused by excessive sweating and purges. While Dr Nikolas Dirx, writing under the name Nikolas Tulp, declared in his *Observationes Medicae*, that 'nothing is comparable to this plant'. Tulp proclaimed tea to be the oldest and best herbal medicine known to the world. However, despite the prolific health claims that tea carried, it remained a cure-all only for the privileged, and even in the 1660s, when the flow of tea importation increased, it remained too expensive to become a drink of the Dutch masses (ale remained the drink of the people). This was despite the large shipments by the East India Company which sent the prices plummeting from a hundred guilders a pound to just ten.

Cornelis Bontekoe (née Dekker) published a paper on tea drinking entitled *Tractaat van het excellenste kruyd Thee* (*Treatise about the most Excellent Herb Tea*) in 1768. The book was controversial amongst many physicians and members of the medical community, who often considered tea drinking a waste of time and money. Bontekoe proudly asserted: 'I have no scruple in advising [people] to drink fifty or a hundred or two hundred cups at a time. I have often drunk as many in a fore- or afternoon, and many people with me, of whom not a single one has died yet.'

Tea purveyors were quick to enlist his help in spreading the good news about their product to customers eager to buy the expensive and exotic concoction. The book sold thousands of copies and was translated into English.

For his enduring promotion of tea, Dr Bontekoe was voted a gratuity as a gesture of appreciation by the grateful Dutch East India Company board of directors. He held tea in such high regard that he advocated drinking it in great volume, recommending that invalids take tea between fifty and a hundred times daily. He attributed many virtues to this panacea drink, including the treatment of malaria, and avidly followed his own advice. He even claimed to have cured himself of stones by drinking tea.

Many British physicians were also taking a curious interest in the health benefits of tea. Thomas Trotter, in his *View of the Nervous Temperament*, argued that tea, as tobacco and coffee, 'had once been used as medicines, but had been reduced to necessities'. As to the causes of mental illness, Trotter dedicated several pages to the hazards of tea, describing it as a 'beverage suited to a indolent and voluptuous age', and while admitting that it could aid in the digestion of heavy meals, he warned that its consumption resulted in 'debility and nervous diseases'.

One of the things that stunted tea's initial popularity and made it spread relatively slowly in Britain was its cost. Regardless of its virtues, it was without doubt a luxury item that was matchless in terms of exclusivity. Two major factors contributed to the cost of tea: the cost of import and taxes. When tea first reached London it had not yet been cultivated in India, so all supplies had to be shipped from China.

Trade was strictly regulated by Chinese officials, with only the Hong Guild licensed to deal with foreign traders. The Chinese were heavily taxed by their own officials, and in turn levied heavy duties on the traders, thus increasing the cost of exported goods. Once tea arrived in Britain, the local government would levy their own taxes and so the cost of tea was high even before merchants could make their profits. Tea importation was also monopolised by the East India Company, meaning that they were free to set the price of tea at whatever rate they fancied without any consideration for competition. It remained a luxury drink throughout the seventeenth century and into the early eighteenth century. Upon its arrival in England tea was initially selling for £3 10 shillings a pound: to put this cost into context, during the seventeenth century the average wage for an agricultural labourer was 8d a day; his wife might get 6d, and children 3d a day.

In 1660, when Samuel Pepys recorded trying tea for the first time, it was still considered unusual in England. This was the first written reference to tea drinking in England, though it was popular in Portugal, Holland and other parts of Europe. On 25 September 1660 Pepys was called to an important meeting with experts in naval affairs, including Sir William Batten, Colonel Slingsby and Sir Richard Ford. He noted: 'To the office, where Sir W. Batten, Colonel Slingsby, and I sat awhile, and Sir. R. Ford coming to us about some business, we talked together of the interest of this kingdom to have peace with Spain and a war with France and Holland: where Sir R. Ford talked like a man of great reason and experience. And afterwards I did send for a cup of tee (a China drink) of which I had never drank before, and went away.'

Sadly, Pepys doesn't give a critique of the tea, but it seems that he did not take to the drink as he made no further mention of it in his diary until seven years later, in 1667, when his wife was prescribed it for medicinal reasons, believing it would be good to remedy her cough: 'Home and found my wife making tea: a drink which Mr Pelling, the potticary, tells her is good for her cold and defluxions.'

Tea was a slow trend to catch on, but catch on it did. It arrived in England around fifty years after the Dutch first brought it to the Netherlands and it was not met with overwhelming fervour. The seventeenth century saw low demand for tea, as its novel status and high price ensured that the only people partaking of the beverage were the wealthy or the nobility.

Catherine of Braganza, consort of King Charles II. Mezzotint by H. H. Quiter after P. Lely, 1678.

While some credit the spread of tea's popularity in Britain to Catherine Braganza, wife of Charles II, she wasn't the first to introduce tea to Britain (Samuel Pepys talked about it two years earlier). Catherine did, however, turn drinking tea into a fad at court and a social habit between her ladies. No doubt those in Catherine's company were captivated by the beauty of the striking porcelain teapots, saucers and cups, and the exotic ritual of making tea. Catherine of Braganza made tea a regular drink at court. The approval of royalty has always carried its own validation, and Catherine's taste for tea spread to the rest of the court. By the late 1600s tea was firmly entrenched in court life and indicative of high social status. The queen's fondness for the beverage could well explain why the directors of the East India Company, when selecting a rare and expensive gift for the King in 1664, opted for one that included 2lb and 2oz of tea.

Tea's new-found fame as a fashionable status symbol was further enhanced at the court of Charles II when Lord Arlington, Secretary of State, and Thomas Butler, Earl of Ossory, returned from The Hague in 1666 with a quantity of tea, which they proceeded to have served in the vogue of aristocratic continental circles. The tea served made quite an impact and Jonas Hanway, an English merchant (who would later author an essay on the dangers of tea, which he blamed for many maladies including scurvy and distemper) made a statement saying that Arlington and Ossory were the first to introduce tea from Holland. This claim was widely echoed, giving Dr Samuel Johnson cause to point out to Hanway that tea had been taxed in England since 1660 and had been sold publicly in London for a few years before that.

The high cost of tea continued to inhibit its widespread, general use, though its popularity at court gave it added appeal to the wealthy and to the apothecaries. Tea would only reach the dizzy heights of mass popularity once the price allowed it.

Today the image of taking tea might conjure up images of elegance and gentility, but tea-drinking initially spread through the male-dominated coffee-house. By 1683 it is said that there were over 2,000 coffee-houses in London alone. There were by this stage various coffee-houses dotted around Cornhill; located in St Michael's Alley was the Virginia, the Senegal and the Jamaica, which frequently enjoyed the patronage of the West Indian traders. In the same alleyway as Garraway's, Exchange Alley, was Jonathon's, where the stock exchange originated, Sam Baker's and The Turk's Head. Coffee-houses of the seventeenth century were nothing like our modern cafés or tea rooms. They were male dominated, and, in the same way that public houses of the twentieth century attracted different types of clientele, so too did the coffee-houses. Men would meet kindred spirits and discuss their own niche interests, with writers, politicians and businessmen all frequenting their own favourite hostelries. The Chapter Coffee House in Paternoster Row was the place for booksellers to meet. In 1688 Edward Lloyd formed a modest coffee-house for seafarers, merchants and underwriters, successfully building up a clientele of shipping merchants from which developed the Lloyd's of London Underwriters.

The coffee-houses around St James's were frequented by those involved in politics and the royal court, and political parties would each meet at rival establishments. Man's Coffee House at Charing Cross was frequented by stockjobbers; White's at St James's, by politicians; Button's in Bow Street, by writers; the Grecian at the Temple and Nando's at the Rainbow Tavern at Inner Temple Lane, by lawyers; Old Slaughter's in St Martin's Lane, by artists; Child's in St Paul's Churchyard, by clergymen; and the Little Devil in Goodman's Fields, by military men. The Amsterdam Coffee House behind the Royal Exchange, where the Hudson Bay Company hired seamen, was founded in 1675. The scientist and surveyor Robert Hooke and his associates met at Garraway's, Jonathan's or Man's. William Urwin opened his new coffee-house at

The interior of a London coffee-house in the seventeenth century.

No 1 Bow Street, on the corner of Russell Street, in 1671, and Will's Coffee House established itself as one of the best-known in London during the period, becoming a favourite of John Dryden, the well-known playwright and poet. Coffee-houses were not just places that served coffee, tea and chocolate, but institutions of debate, news and enterprise.

Forget images of modern coffee-shops with their velveteen seats and designer décor, coffee-houses were simple debating houses, where playwrights, journalists and members of the public gathered around wooden tables drinking, thinking, writing and discussing literature into the night. Coffee-houses were places that brought men and ideas together. They were all unique and well beyond our imagination as places where we would buy our precision-made speciality teas or frothy coffees.

No two coffee-houses were the same. Each had its own ambience and character, from those that closely resembled a private club to others where men argued and chewed tobacco, but they all followed the same formula, maximising the interaction between customers and forging a creative, convivial environment. The coffee-house came to occupy a central place in seventeenth- and eighteenth-century English culture and commerce. As with taverns, before the introduction of the postal service, coffee-houses also acted as post offices for sending or receiving letters, further enhancing their function as a business hub.

Some would say they offered an alternative to rowdy taverns and ale houses, but it's important not to think of coffee-houses as bubbles of civility, where men of all classes could evade the harsh, rough and tumble of the city. This would be an inaccurate description. Many coffee-houses could be noisy and boisterous places. Upon entering, patrons would often be engulfed in smoke and raucous debate. Rows of well-dressed men in periwigs would sit around rectangular wooden tables strewn with every type of media imaginable: newspapers, pamphlets, prints, manuscript newsletters, ballads, even party-political playing cards. Sometimes coffee-houses were characterised by coarseness, earthy behaviour and casual violence, while others became notorious haunts of London's low life.

Tom King's Coffee House was an old night-house of Covent Garden Market that was open in the early hours of the morning when the market trading began. It was run by Moll and Tom, a pair of colourful characters. Moll King, whose real name was Elizabeth Adkins, had more than her fair share of dalliances with the law and an equal share of lovers and paying customers along the way. Meanwhile, Tom King was born into a socially acceptable and financially solvent family, and was Eton-educated, albeit until his expulsion. He took up work in Covent Garden Market and soon became locally known as 'Smooth'd-Fac'd-Tom'.

Elizabeth Adkins originated from the nearby slum district of St Giles, and was more than a petty thief and prostitute; she was an entrepreneur who, from the age of fourteen, had supplemented her income on the streets of London's seedy heartland. After finding the prospect of a life spent in service unappealing, she entered a life she'd grown up with; hawking fruit and vegetables in Covent Garden. Though of dubious moral character, she was reported to be an extraordinary pickpocket, a thief and a prostitute. During her criminal career she had at least twelve known aliases, changing her surname as it suited. Between 1697 and 1713 alone, 'Mary King' was indicted on eleven separate charges, though this by no means represented the whole of her offenses. When she ran the coffee-house with her husband she didn't turn her back on her life of crime, she just operated under a different guise, including that of a loan shark.

The coffee-house began selling alcohol as its long opening hours meant there was an opportunity to attract those wanting something a little stronger than tea or coffee. It attracted plenty of customers and was described as being 'well known to all gentlemen to whom beds are unknown'. King's Coffee House became popular with revellers and a hub for those with immoral conduct in mind. It was described by Fielding in one of his prologues as follows: 'what rake is ignorant of King's Coffee House?'

In an historical context a rake was a man who led a wild, dissipated life or else a rogue or scoundrel who fully indulged in all the sensual pleasures life had to offer. With a good patronage of rakes, the 'King's College', as the coffee-house was affectionately known, became a brothel of sorts. The coffee-house was ideally located for such activities. Covent Garden was well known as being the site of London's most important flower and vegetable market by day, and a place to find sins of the flesh by night, and its sordid nightly uses were well publicised. At King's, libertines could sober up after a long night of drinking and revelry, passing the time by browsing a directory of prostitutes before being led to the requisite brothel on nearby Bow Street. Tom and Moll King cleverly ensured that only the introduction between the prostitute and client took place on their premises, and because there were no beds in the building no charges could be brought against them. Business boomed and as the liquor, tea and other exotic

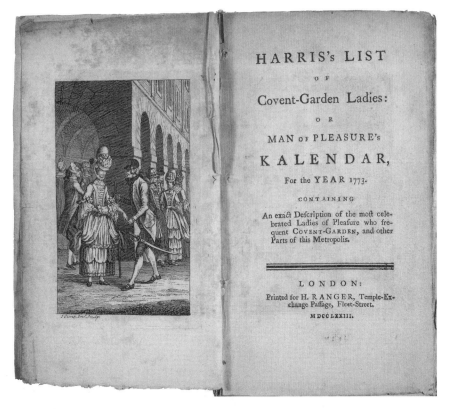

A Pocketbook Guide to Prostitutes - Harris's List of Covent Garden Ladies, published some time between 1757 and 1795.

beverages flowed, so too did the popularity of this coffee-house grow. It was frequented by market workers and those of the highest social rank alike and it attracted the attention of many reformers who attempted in vain to shut it down.

Tom King indulged and revelled too enthusiastically with his customers and died in 1737 from an illness exacerbated by drink. Moll took over the reigns of the business and her witty disposition meant that the coffee-house continued to be well frequented. With her colourful past and natural leaning towards scandal and debauchery, Moll King was often fined for keeping a disorderly house, but despite this she amassed a good fortune and the jolly antics of King's Coffee House were recorded forever in Hogarth's scene 'The Morning', in which the artist depicts some of the frolics and cavorting of King's Coffee House clientele, while at the door there is a drunken row in full swing.

There was even a floating coffee-house known as the Folly of the Thames, moored outside Somerset House. This coffee-house offered a stark contrast to today's rash of sterile coffee-shop chains. It started life as a fashionable haven for socialites, but descended into a raunchy melting pot of late-night revelry. During its time as a fashionable floating entertainment venue, Pepys paid it more than one visit, as he tells us in his diary, and on one occasion it was honoured by a visit from

An illustration of the Folly on the Thames, 1842.

Queen Mary and several of her courtiers. However, it took a dive in standards when 'unprincipled' women were admitted and soon became notorious as a house of debauchery, where unrestrained drinking, promiscuous dancing and acts of disrepute took place. Tom D'Urfey's song, *A Touch of the Times* (1719), alludes to The Folly: 'When Drapers' smugg'd apprentices, With Exchange girls mostly jolly, After shop was shut up and all, Could sail up to The Folly.' It was described by satirist Tom Brown thus, 'This whimsical piece of architecture was designed as a musical summer-house for the entertainment of the quality, where they might meet and ogle one another.' The Folly enjoyed an outrageous reputation as a place where dancers performed late into the night and bawdy entertainment abounded, but eventually it fell into scandalous decay and died a shameful death.

Coffee-houses became the haunts of hustlers and deceivers, and visitors were warned to be cautious. Sir John Fielding warned that a 'stranger or a foreigner' should exercise caution when visiting:

> The deceivers of this denomination are generally descended from families of some repute, have had the groundwork of a gented education, and are capable of making a tolerable appearance. Having been equally profuse of their own substance and character and learned, by having been undone, the ways of undoing, they lie in wait for those who have more wealth and less knowledge of the town [...] they insinuate themselves into the company and acquaintance of strangers, whom they watch every opportunity of fleecing.
>
> And if one finds you in the least inclination to cards, dice, the billiard table, bowling green, or any other sort of gaming, you are morally sure of being taken in.
>
> For this set of gentry are adepts in all the arts of knavery and tricking.
>
> Sir John Fielding (magistrate), *Description of London and Westminster*, 1776

While some coffee-houses gained dubious reputations there is no disputing that many inspired brilliant ideas, even discoveries, that led to Britain becoming the envy of the world. Conversation and debate was their lifeblood and Samuel Pepys recorded fantastical tales of voyages

(51)

Mifs Gr—n, No. 32, *Little Ruffel-ftreet.*

Strait a new heat return'd with his embrace,
Warmth to my blood and colour to my face;
Till at the length, with mutual kiffes fir'd,
To the laft blifs we eagerly afpir'd,
And both alike attain'd, what both alike
    defir'd.

When beauty beats up for recruits, he
muft be an errant coward indeed, who re-
fufes to enlift under its banner; and
when good humour, complaifance, and
engaging behaviour are the rewards of
fervice, it is fhameful to defert. This
lady's charms attract moft who behold
them; though of a low ftature, and
rather under the middle fize, fhe is ele-
gantly formed; her black eyes, contrafted
with her white teeth, are highly pleafing,
and the goodnefs of her temper rivets the
chains which her agreeable form firft put
on. One guinea, is then, too poor a re-
compence for fuch merit; and it is to be
deplored, that a girl, who fhould only
exchange love for love, fhould be obliged
to take payment for what is ever beyond
price: in bed, fhe is by far the better
                    E 2   piece,

Extract from Harris's List which listed 120-190 female prostitutes working
in Georgian London.

31

'across the high hills in Asia above the clouds', and of metaphysical discussions on the futility of distinguishing between a waking and a dreaming state.

The coffee-house became so important that neither the plague years (1664-1665), nor the Great Fire of London in 1666 diminished their growth. In fact, the rapid reconstruction of the Royal Exchange by 1669 was accompanied by the launch of many new coffee-houses.

With so many men meeting and discussing the affairs of the day, Lord Danby, the King's chief minister from 1674, was wary of the rise of coffee-houses, considering them a hotbed of political intrigue where opponents of Charles II distributed their inflammatory pamphlets. In 1675 he issued a proclamation ordering their closure, but the plan had to be abandoned because it caused so much resentment. Besides, there was by then such a large stock of tea and coffee in London that banning them would have caused commercial problems for many of their proprietors.

Despite the considerable revenues gained from the excise duties and licensing of coffee-houses, they faced an image problem. Charles II considered them to be a dangerous source of subversive activities, centres for dissemination of seditious rumours and material. Charles II and the Earl of Clarendon were fully aware that James Harrington's Republican Rota Club was regularly meeting at Miles' Coffee House in London, even after the restoration of the monarchy had been assured, but of graver concern was the role of coffee-houses as hubs for political debate and news that made the managers of the Restoration regime sit uneasily.

The Licensing Act of 1662 gave the secretaries of state a monopoly on the printing of news. The *London Gazette* soon became acknowledged as the official publication of Britain. While the state had the monopoly of news in principal, that was all it could boast, because in reality unofficial news was flourishing.

In 1666 Charles II looked into the possibility of banning coffee-houses by Royal Proclamation, but the Secretary of State, William Coventry, argued that the excise duties were valuable and that such a ban might stir up greater animosity and resentment against the Crown. They were, however, such busy centres of news and intelligence that it was felt action had to be taken. But instead of taking direct action against the coffee-houses themselves, the Privy Council issued an order banning the sale of printed works to the hawkers who sold materials there. However, it wasn't long before the Crown was once again considering direct action against the coffee-houses.

By February 1671 the king was consulting the privy council about whether there was an effective way of suppressing them and wanted to put in place an outright ban. Once again, though, his plans did not find favour, but the king instructed his attorney general, Sir Heneage Finch, to draft a proclamation against coffee-house rumour-mongering and in June he duly issued a royal proclamation to such effect: 'command all his loveing subjects of what [ever] state or sondition soe may be, from the highest to the lowest, that they [shall not] utter or publish any false newes or reports or intermeddle with the affaires of state and government, or with the persons of any of his Majesties counsellors or ministers in their common and ordinary discourses.'

Information on subversive news being spread throughout the kingdom's coffee-houses flooded into the secretary of state's office. Rumours escalated regarding the third Anglo-Dutch War and in May 1674 the king issued another proclamation against the practice of false news and licentious rumour-mongering against the state and government. Not long after this, in 1675, a document began to circulate around the coffee-houses. Entitled 'A letter from a Person of Quality to his Friend in the Country', it was quickly and correctly labeled as 'the Manifesto of the Whig Party'. Within its pages the court was accused of falling victim to a faction of churchmen and cavaliers who wished to propagate popery in religion and an absolutist state into the kingdom.

Understandably, the House of Lords ordered the work to be destroyed and the identities of the author, printers and distributors revealed. The 'manifesto' was made illegal and thus became a more interesting and sought-after read with an increased price to reflect this.

The king tried to ban coffee-houses again and this time gathered the support of his council. On 29 December 1675 Charles II declared that after 10 January 1676 it would be forbidden to sell by retail, 'any coffee, chacolet, sherbet or tea'. Licences were revoked and the proclamation was published in the *London Gazette*.

The most significant opposition came from the coffee-house proprietors who claimed that the proclamation was denying them an innocent living and causing them unfair hardship. The king was presented with a petition on 6 January 1676 and Charles met with his Privy Council and an assembly of legal experts in order to assess and debate the matter further.

The council considered the legality of the king's actions in consideration of the licenses that were still valid at the time of the proclamation and the question arose as to whether the Crown could legitimately revoke licenses that had been granted legally and complied with. It seemed that Charles' proclamation stood on shaky legal ground and now a solution that did not look like bowing down had to be put in place. This came in the form of a six-month reprieve, which stated that coffee-houses could remain open until 24 June 1676, so that their keepers could attempt to sell off their existing stocks and supplies.

The coffee-house keepers, as part of this reprieve, were enjoined that they would not accept any 'scandalous papers, books of libels' into their establishments. By midsummer the reprieve was over and it was reiterated that all coffee-houses were to be extinguished.

The battle between the Crown and the coffee-houses raged long after the failure to push through a ban in January 1676. King Charles II did not reinstate his demand for a full suppression in midsummer 1676 and instead issued another license of extension.

The 'reformed' coffee-houses continued to operate, but the pretence was short-lived and the business of scandal and news was soon booming again. The court's failure to secure outright suppression meant that self-proclaimed 'liberty defenders' were soon spreading 'news' as before.

In October 1676 a plan to engage in a naval expedition against the pirates of Algiers was abandoned because it transpired that the plans of the attack had been leaked to London coffee-houses. The issue of licensing coffee-houses consequently reared its head again. When the second licensing extension expired in January 1677, Charles II was again interested in the possibility of quashing the troublesome coffee-house. After all, following the Algiers leak the king was unlikely to be as lenient.

With the threat to coffee-house operations in play once again, a group of leading proprietors once more petitioned the king, pleading with him to allow them to practice their trade. Charles accepted their petition, but added a proviso, 'if at any time hereafter [...] the petitioners or any of them have misbehaved themselves or not punctually observed their [...] promise and engagement [not to accept libels or scandalous discourse]', he warned of his right to rescind 'his gracious favour and indulgence to them'.

Charles II never fully abandoned his wish to abolish coffee-houses and in December 1679 the idea of abolition was floated in the Privy Council. Again the ghosts of 1675 and 1676 were raised and the same lobbying effort by coffee-house keepers was mobilised. They effectively argued that such a ban would deprive great numbers of honest men of a living and that the sale of tea, coffee, sherbet and chocolate was an innocent trade rather than a seditious one.

In 1688 King James II of England, Charles II's successor, revealed that he was as displeased by the existence of coffee-houses as his predecessor. He demanded that licenses be refused to all coffee-house keepers who did not adhere to providing a security fee to guarantee they would not keep or sanction the presence of unlicensed books or papers on their premises. He banned the distribution of any newspapers in coffee-houses (other than the official state paper, the *London Gazette*) as a measure designed principally to prevent the circulation of publications believed to be critical or detrimental to the stability of the state.

When the legislation controlling the publication of newspapers generally lapsed in 1695, several periodicals were launched in London (usually published two or three times a week), catering to the insatiable demand for fresh information. It is certain that unofficial news and publications had continued to flourish throughout the ban, albeit under the cover of darkness. In the long term the Crown reluctantly lived with coffee-houses and James II was the last monarch to issue a Royal Proclamation prohibiting the

An illustration of Garraway's Coffee-House.

dissemination of unofficial news and political propaganda in the coffee-houses. All through the remaining years of the seventeenth century and into most of the eighteenth century, coffee-houses prospered and the sales of tea increased. Despite their name they did much to promote the drinking of tea, which was associated with free speech and peace. Indeed in Andrew Marvel's satirical attack on Charles II's proclamation in his poem, 'A Dialogue Between Two Horses' (1676), he concludes that while drinking tea is associated with free speech and peace, the royalist toasts in ale, wine and brandy only lead to treason:

> It is wine and strong drinks makes tumults increase;
> Choc'late, tea and coffee are liquors of peace:
> No quarrels nor oaths amongst those that drink'em;
> 'Tis Bachus and brewers swear, damn 'em, and sink 'em!
> Then, Charles, thy edicts against coffee recall:
> There's ten times more treason in brandy and ale.'

Tea remained a luxury beverage enjoyed by the elite throughout the seventeenth and early eighteenth centuries, but it was slowly infusing its way into English life. The great surge of tea importation and the consequent drop in price from the 1730s onwards was set to make the British love affair with this exotic brew strong and enduring.

If we briefly look at the wages and the cost of tea during the early eighteenth century we can see that it was beginning to enter an affordable price range. In the early eighteenth century the average laborer earned between 16d and 18d per day[1]. An entire crate of cheap Bohea tea sold at approximately 5 shillings, or five days' work[2]. It is certain that tea prices were falling, but the cost was still prohibitive to the middle and lower classes. Despite a desire for tea, they simply could not financially afford to enjoy tea on a daily basis.

The surge in tea importation and the consequent drop in price came soon after the direct clipper trade to China was opened. It was not until the end of the eighteenth century that tea would become a relatively inexpensive and readily available commodity. Consumption increased dramatically during the eighteenth century when it began circulating through the middle and lower classes. It was estimated by Sir George Staunton at the end of the eighteenth century that tea was consumed at a rate of 'more than a pound weight each, in the course of a year, for the individuals of all ranks, ages and sexes.'

As a pound of tea can be expected to yield between 200 and 300 cups, in accordance with Sir Staunton's estimations adults were consuming at least two cups of tea per day. Though in reality unofficial imports of tea were increasing and there are some suggestions that as much tea reached England illegally as it did legitimately.

The increase in tea's popularity was only partially due to increasing availability. The decline in tea's exclusivity to the upper class is reflected in the sharp increase in tea imports from the 1730s to the middle of the century. The amount of tea imported represents far more than the aristocracy and elite could drink alone. Tea was set to become a staple of the British daily diet.

Not surprisingly, however, as tea's popularity increased it would soon become a target for smugglers, profiteers and swindlers. Tea was set for mass consumption and was about to become part of British culture.

Finding calm in a teacup...

Chapter 3

Tea Demand: Opium, Slums and Prostitutes

The demand for tea rose rapidly from the mid-seventeenth century. The amount drunk per person was increasing and Britain was destined to become enslaved to the exotic beverage. The demand was fulfilled by the East India Company, which placed its first order in 1664: 100lb of China tea to be shipped from Java to Britain. This increased in the 1720s with average imports rising to around 900,000lb per annum and then increasing to 3.7 million lb in the 1750s.

The East India Company imported four main types of tea. The cheapest was Bohea, which was made from the coarser, more mature leaves. Then there were the finer grades, which included Congo, Souchon and the highest grade, Pekoe, made from the most select young leaf buds. The most popular type was Bohea, which, as sales grew, became affordable even to the lower classes by the middle of the eighteenth century. In 1736 an anonymous poem, entitled, 'In Praise of Tea', sums up its socioeconomic status:

> When tea was sold for guineas by the pound,
> The poor a drinking Tea were never found,
> Then only china dishes cou'd be bought.
> Burnt in with gold, or else in colours wrought:
> Now tea is cheap, so dishes are same;
> The pray wherein are they so much blame.

The rise of tea's popularity was in part due to the rise of disposable income in all classes, meaning that small luxuries, including tea, could now be afforded. The rising cost of beer due to the malt taxes also made tea a more enticing proposition, but the enormous push given to tea promotion by the East India Company cannot be underestimated.

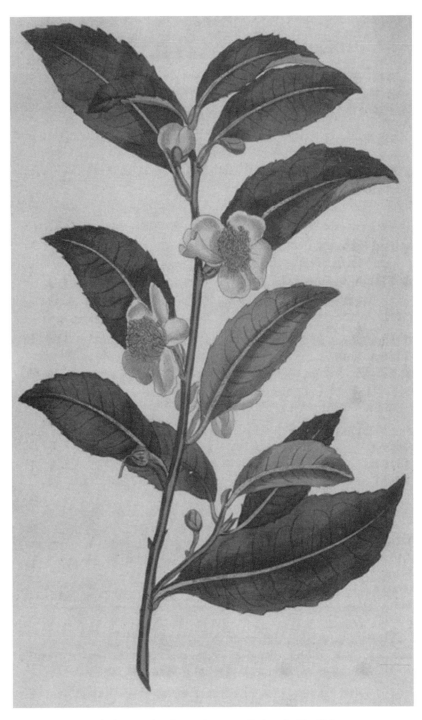

Wuyi tea, formerly known by the trade name Bohea in English.

Tea was not an immediate success in Britain. Coffee flourished and was better established as the luxury hot drink of choice, but tea was easier to prepare and, moreover, Britain had interests in the Far East where tea grew and thus was promoted by the powerful East India Company. The government saw tea as an important source of revenue and pushed tea far more than coffee (though it must be noted that cocoa also received a good dose of promotion through advertising in the nineteenth century).

The East India Trading Company held the monopoly on tea trade from 1661 until 1834, and in 1717 they finally won the right to trade directly with Canton, thus increasing imports of tea dramatically. The East India Company, popularly called the John Company, originated in 1600. Its origins lay in the growing opportunities for global trade resulting from the decline of Spanish naval power after 1588. The void left by the destruction of the Spanish Armada would soon be filled by other countries, with England and the Netherlands being first among them. Over the next few years, England and the Netherlands surpassed the rest of their competition and by 1600 the English fleet had gained enough ships and navigational skill to allow it to figure prominently in the trade relationship with the East Indies. The distances involved in trading proved prohibitive to most, as ships were the only method of importing goods. Queen Elizabeth I, who had a powerful navy and a taste for the exotic, allowed the formation of the East India Company for the purpose of trade with India and the acquisition of rare and luxury goods. This was not just about wealth for Elizabeth I, but about keeping up appearances. The spectacle of wealth and finery sent a message of success to her British subjects and to the wider world.

The formation of the East India Company ensured that a steady flow of exotic foreign wares flowed into British ports, with the monarchy and the privileged able to garner status from the possession of the new and unfamiliar. The charter which established the East India Company provided it with previously unheard of powers for a private company. Elizabeth had created it as an instrument for all foreign trade, with branches in the East Indies, the Americas, and continental Europe.

After being granted a monopoly on trade to the East Indies in 1661, the Company acquired many of the powers usually confined to the British government, along with the authority to use them. In 1661 Charles II not only renewed the Company's charter, but also granted it a second monopoly on all British trade in the East, including China. By 1693 trade with the Chinese was off to a slow but determined start, and attempts were made to establish permanent contacts.

Before 1600 Portugal had controlled most European trade with India and the Far East, but once established the East India Company soon began competing with the Portuguese for trading opportunities. The Company's first major base was in western India, where it found a rich source of exotic textiles and other produce that could be exported back to Britain or taken further east to exchange for spices.

Britain needed more tea and as demand rose so imports had to keep up. Tea from China kept the West contented but by the eighteenth century the amount consumed in Britain had increased dramatically, and with it trade tensions between China and the East India Company. Paying for the relatively small quantities of tea being imported had not been a problem for Britain. They purchased it with silver and Indian cotton, but as China's cotton production became more refined they no longer needed cheap Indian cotton. As Britain's thirst for tea grew, the worry was that too much silver was leaving England's coffers. After 1770 it was no longer practicable to use silver to pay for tea, as the cost had risen due to inflation, while Mexico (a main source for silver) was cut off due to the American Revolution. The demand for tea was higher than ever, but the money was not there to pay for it. The solution that the Company came up with was simply to exchange tea for a far more addictive drug.

In 1758 Parliament gave the East India Trading Company the monopoly on the production of opium in India. Though the import of opium into China was prohibited, Portugal was engaged in the illegal import of the drug. By 1776, however, the Company had taken control and was influential in the export of sixty tons of opium to China. The production and export of opium to China had become a mass operation, employing nearly a million people in Bengal for growing purposes, and by 1830 some 1500 tons had been exported to China. Officially there was no connection between the East India Company's monopoly on tea and its monopoly on opium: the Company sold opium to British merchants in India, who then took it to China where corrupt officials handled it. The merchants received silver coins for the opium consignments which were then sold back to the East India Company. This silver made its way back to London where it was given to those who went to China to buy the tea on behalf of the Company. This opium-silver-tea triangle was a lucrative one, both for the East India Company and the British Crown, but it was having a detrimental effect on China.

Britain was not immune from the grip of the opium trade. Opium dens were springing up in London and in other ports where the drug was landed alongside other cargo from all over the empire. The expansionist nature of the Victorian British Empire meant that new interactions between people and goods were always possible.

Opium and other narcotic drugs played an important part in Victorian life and in a way that we would find shocking and hard to understand today. Strychnine, arsenic and cyanide were often concealed in chemist's tonics and over-the-counter recipes, while opium use was viewed very differently to the way it is today. Chemists regularly sold laudanum and other opium preparations, as well as cocaine and arsenic, and opium sellers included stationers, tobacconists and barbers.

The availability of opium in London and other port cities and towns was linked to the East India Company's growth and cultivation of the drug in India, from where it bled into China. Given that the majority of the world's opium production was in India, and governed

An opium-den in the east end of London.

by a British company, it is not surprising that the drug found its way into British ports.

Indeed, if you were observing a British port in the eighteenth or nineteenth century you would have seen opium arriving in plain sight alongside ordinary cargo. In February 1785 *The Times* listed opium from Smyrna (now Izmir) amongst other consignments of oil from Leghorn (Livorno) and peas from Dantzic (Gdansk). In the early nineteenth century visitors to Norfolk were heeded a warning to treat their pint of ale with caution as it could be laced with opium to ward off the malaria that flourished in the Fens at the time.

Opium has many derivatives including morphine, codeine, oxycodone and heroin. The Victorian era, which is often depicted as being prudish and restrained, actually saw narcotics being used for pleasure to a high degree. The austerity of nineteenth-century British life was perhaps the reason why so many Victorians sought escape through these drugs. For the lowest ranks of society, life was wracked with poverty and inequality. A typical view of urban horror is provided by John Ruskin: 'That great foul city of London — rattling, growling, smoking, stinking — ghastly heap of fermenting brickwork, pouring out poison at every pore.' The promotion of drugs by industries such as pharmaceutical tonics, tobacco, tea, coffee and alcohol provided this escapism and comfort with various herbal infusions and decoctions. The Victorian pharmacy was a place few would recognise today, selling not only patent and proprietary medicines, but also home-made nostrums and raw ingredients for the making of home remedies.

There was a well-established tradition of including opium in products intended for the treatment of infants. Such opiate-laced preparations were even used for minor ailments such as colic or wind. Godfrey's Cordial contained tincture of opium and molasses and was a popular preparation for the 'soothing' of infants.

During the 1840s officials began to raise concerns about the prevalent use of preparations containing opium for the treatment of 'Disorders of Children'. The reported mortality rates were scandalous and there were many contemporary newspaper reports of infant mortalities due to the administration of opiate-based tinctures. Thomas Bull, in his 'Hints to Mothers' (1854), estimated that three-quarters of all deaths from opiate decoctions occurred in children under five years.

The most common way that Godfrey's Cordial caused infant fatality was through overdose. This was generally considered to be accidental,

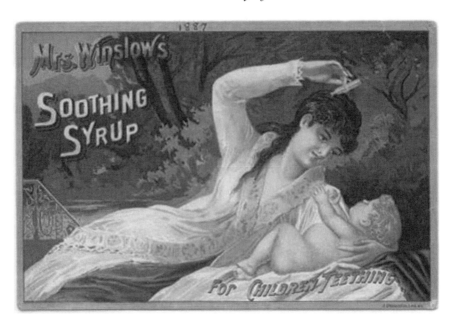

Above: An 1887 advert for Mrs. Winslow's Soothing Syrup - it's primary ingredients were morphine and alcohol.

Left: Godfrey's Cordial - a popular, opiate-based children's tonic.

but in some cases it may have been a way of keeping the size of poverty-stricken families under control in a time before reliable contraception. Starvation was another result of babies being given Godfrey's Cordial. Newborns were doped-up on opiates and failed to wake in order to feed and gain the nutrients they needed.

On the advertising for Ayer's Cherry Pectoral, children beam angelically in nostalgic innocence, but the mixture was one of alcohol and opium that would now be considered a poison. And while children were sedated with opium-based tonics, the adults took opium pills, which were coated in varnish for lower classes and silver or gold for the wealthy.

Meanwhile, the chemists did a roaring trade in drugs for every ailment, from laudanum for dysentery to chlorodyne for influenza and camphorated tincture of opium for asthma. The use of opiates was widespread and home remedies for coughs and colds that included laudanum mixed with treacle were common. John Wesley, who was better known for his religious work, wrote a book of medicine, entitled *Primitive Physic, Or, An Easy and Natural Way of Curing Most Diseases* (1761). In it he offers a recipe for cold medicine that he calls 'oily emulsion'. Its ingredients are listed as: six ounces of salt water, two drams of volatile aromatic spirit, an ounce of Florence oil, and half an ounce of sugar syrup. The elixir is essentially a mixture of camphor and opium.

Thomas Sydenham, the pioneering seventeenth-century doctor, had a recipe that contained 'one pint of sherry wine, two ounces of good-quality Indian or Egyptian opium, one of saffron, a cinnamon stick and a clove, both powdered'. In other period recipes, fruit juice, sugar, various spices and opium were fermented into alcoholic syrups. Even *Mrs Beeton's Household Management* had recipes for opium-based remedies.

The trade in over-the-counter opiates, however, was not just supplying those in need of cold remedies or looking to soothe a baby's teething. Instead, they were used to mollify the bitter reality of the sweat, noise, filth and debauchery of Victorian London for the city's unfortunates.

'The Maiden Tribute of Modern Babylon I: the Report of our Secret Commission', published in the *Pall Mall Gazette* in July 1885, was W.T. Stead's shocking exposé of young girls forced into London brothels. It revealed in graphic and scandalous detail how young and under-privileged girls were being entered into a criminal underworld of brothels, drugs and abuse, where wealthy paedophiles could revel

A nineteenth century advert for Ayer's Cherry Pectoral, made from an opium derivative.

'in the cries of an immature child'. While the recruitment of young girls into sex work may not appear to immediately involve opium, Stead explains, 'Some [young girls] are simply snared, trapped and outraged either when under the influence of drugs or after a prolonged struggle in a locked room, in which the weaker succumbs to sheer downright force.' Drugs, especially laudanum, were not only used by prostitutes to blot out the misery of their daily lives but also in the initiation of a girl's downfall into prostitution, as this passage reveals:

> A gentleman paid me £13 for the first of her, soon after she came to town. She was asleep when he did it – sound asleep. To tell the truth, she was drugged. It is often done. I gave her a drowse. It is a mixture of laudanum and something else. Sometimes chloroform is used, but I always used either snuff or laudanum. We call it drowse or black draught, and they lie almost as if dead, and the girl never knows what has happened till morning. And then? Oh! Then she cries a great deal from pain, but she is 'mazed, and hardly knows what has happened except that she can hardly move from pain. Of course we tell her it is all right; all girls have to go through it some time, that she is through it now without knowing it, and that it is no use crying. It will never be undone for all the crying in the world. She must now do as the others do.
>
> 'The Maiden Tribute of Modern Babylon I: the Report of our Secret Commission'

Opiates were also employed in baby farming, the practice of accepting custody of an infant in exchange for payment. Baby farming was common in Victorian England, fuelled by society's intolerance of desperate single mothers whose perceived immorality meant they were barred from the workhouse and their ruin was sealed if they kept their child. They had very few options: enter into prostitution, starve or dispose of their baby. Abortion was illegal and backstreet abortions were expensive and risky; abandonment was illegal and murder carried the death penalty. Baby farming offered a simple and legal alternative and carried the rose-tinted hope that their baby would have a future. Mothers responded to adverts placed by baby farmers that offered safe and suitable homes for infants in exchange for them paying a fee.

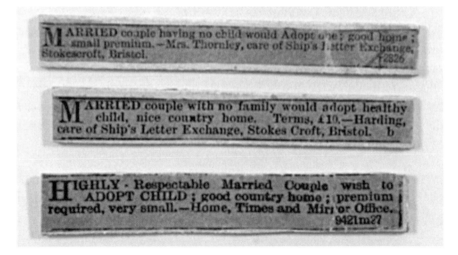

Fake adoption advertisements placed by Amelia, the Reading baby farmer.

Sadly, some baby farmers found it easier to kill the babies entrusted to their care than to rehome them. Take, for instance, the infamous Amelia Dyer who placed adverts promising a better future for unplanned babies: 'Married couple with no family would adopt healthy child, nice country home. Terms - £10.' Once in receipt of her fee, and instead of providing the baby a decent home, Dyer would murder them, either by drugging them with an opiate-laced cordial known as Mother's Friend, starving them or else by strangulation. There were plenty of other baby farmers, including Annie Walters, who would asphyxiate babies with chlorodyne, or Margaret Waters who administered fatal doses of laudanum to the young infants that fell into her care.

Tales of opium dens in London must have been startling and frightening to polite Victorian society. Dark tales of drugs and loose morals circulated and today when we think about opium and the Victorians it's easy to conjure up images of John Chinaman in Dickens' *The Mystery of Edwin Drood*, of the dark shadows looming in London's dismal East End. Yet the real threat was not the London slums or mysterious opium dens run by immigrants: opium was available without restriction. Opium was the aspirin of its day, available cheaply at every chemist and grocer's shop, without the need for medical prescription. Without ready access to medical care, opium and its derivatives (laudanum, paregoric) were superlative remedies for fevers, aches, pains, the dying, the desolate and the mad. Cheaper than gin or wine, opium-laced products offered a welcome escape for those on life's edge.

Nevertheless, the popular fictionalised accounts of the likes of Sax Rohmer and Thomas Burke telling of the exploits of dubious Chinese immigrants intent on world domination created an unjustified fear. As a result, Limehouse in East London came to hold a dangerous and sinister reputation, in which Chinese men fraternised with young white women and smoked opium. In its full form, the East End Chinese 'opium den', with its trappings of drug addiction and easy sexuality, only really existed in the overactive imaginations of novelists. However, in this area of Chinese shops and restaurants, laundries and lodging houses sprang up to cater for the needs of a growing community, and this did include the social consumption of opium. Add to the mix the overcrowded streets of Limehouse, with its brothels catering for the maritime trade, slum housing and poverty, and you have all the ingredients for a dangerous and exaggerated reputation. Unsurprisingly, public opinion of the Chinese immigrants, who were mainly employed in seafaring, was less than flattering. An article entitled 'Fragments of China', written by G.W. Ward and published by *The Windsor Magazine* in 1896, gave a forthright account of the author's low opinion of the Chinese, 'Frankly I dislike the yellow race: deceitful, inhuman and obstinate.' Ward goes on to highlight that 'The untravelled Englishman depends mostly for his views regarding China and its people upon the heathen whom he sees around the East-End.' It is certain that the British opinion of the Chinese had shifted from that of an exotic and cultured people to a nation of drug addicted crooks. An account of the opium dens in China, published on 20 November 1858 in the *Illustrated London News*, must have further fuelled the fears and prejudices of its readers, who no doubt sipped their tea from China while contemplating the terrible effects of Chinese opium addiction:

> The rooms where the Chinese sit and smoke opium are surrounded by wooden couches with places for the head to rest upon and generally a side room devoted for gambling. The pipe is a reed of about an inch in diameter [....] The drug is prepared with some kind of incense and a very small portion is sufficient to charge it, one or two whiffs being the utmost that can be inhaled from a single pipe; and the smoke is taken into the lungs as from the bookals in India.
>
> A few days of this fearful luxury, when taken to excess, will impart a pallid and haggard look to the features, and

a few months, or even weeks, will change the strong and healthy man into little better than an idiot-skeleton.

In the hours devoted to their ruin, these infatuated people may be seen at nine o'clock in the evening, in all the different stages. Some entering half distracted, to feed the craving appetite they have been obliged to subdue during the day, others laughing and talking under the effect of the pipe, whilst the couches around are filled with their different occupants who lie languid, while an idiot smile upon their countenance proves them to be completely under the influence of the drug to passing events, and last emerging into the wished for consummation.

The last scene in this tragic play is generally in a room in the rear of the building, a species of morgue, or dead house, where lie those who have passed into the state of bliss the opium-smoker madly seeks – an emblem of the long sleep to which he is blindly hurrying.

This unsettling account highlighted the serious social consequences of opium smoking in China. Opium was nothing new in the country.

An illustration of a Chinese opium den.

During the Middle Ages Arab and Turkish traders had taken opium to China and India, where it was traded for medicinal purposes to treat conditions such as nervousness and for pain relief. It was soon found that those prescribed opium became addicted, though this addiction was nothing compared to the increase of addiction that was to come as a result of the vast quantities of opium imported to finance tea exports to Britain. In the nineteenth century China adopted the practice of mixing opium with tobacco and smoking it, thus significantly increasing the demand for this drug.

The dramatic increase in the practice of smoking opium began to have serious social and economic consequences for China. Emperor Daoguang (1782-1850) placed Lin Zexu as special Imperial Commissioner to tackle the problem. Lin Zexu attempted to eradicate the opium trade.

The British ignored the Chinese pleas to halt the flow of opium into the country. Money was at stake and the British did not want to jeopardise the profitable opium-silver-tea business triangle, so they simply ignored China's appeals. The India-China opium trade was very important to the British economy; they had increased the export a thousand times over in the fifty years leading up to the 1830s. The British government was also making a huge profit from the import and sale of tea. While the British addiction to tea increased, in China the drug described by Thomas De Quincey as leading into an 'abyss of divine enjoyment' caused grave concern. The number of opium addicts grew 'day by day', noted one emperor.

The flow of opium into China created not only mass addiction in the population but also political instability. In a determined effort to tackle the opium problem, Lin Zexu ordered police raids and the destruction of opium stashes. In 1839 he wrote to Queen Victoria stating, 'Your Majesty has not before been thus officially notified, and you may plead ignorance of the severity of our laws, but I now give my assurance that we mean to cut this harmful drug forever.' Queen Victoria never received this letter as it was rejected by Charles Elliot, Chief Superintendent of British trade in China, on the grounds of addressing the Queen on equal diplomatic terms. And so tensions continued to swell.

In 1840 Lin wrote a second letter to Queen Victoria, signed by the emperor, which was entrusted to Captain Warner of the *Thomas Coutts*: 'Where is your conscience? I have heard that the smoking of opium is very strictly forbidden by your country [...] Since it is not permitted to do harm to your own country, then even less should you let it be passed on

Portrait of Lin Zexu.

to the harm of other countries – how much less to China.' Lin's second letter reached England, but was rejected by Palmerston in the Foreign Office, because Captain Warner had signed Lin's bond. The letter never reached the Queen or anyone in the British government.

China's patience had run out. The unlawful smuggling of opium had been taking place in Chinese ports for over a century and Commissioner Lin Zexu was determined to eradicate the opium trade in Canton once and for all. Official tensions between the Qing government and British representatives escalated soon after Lin demonstrated his serious intent to stamp out the opium imports. Following several unsuccessful edicts to ban the imports in 1839, the commissioner blockaded the Canton port, keeping foreign merchants, who were mainly British, under house arrest until they surrendered their chests of opium for destruction. Under these orders over 1,000 tons of opium was confiscated from mainly British dealers in Canton. The dealers and interested parties were outraged, and counting their financial losses, they pressured their government back in London into demanding that Beijing repay them the full street value of their seized narcotics. When the emperor refused these demands Britain declared war on China over questions of trade, diplomacy, national dignity and, most importantly, drug trafficking. While British officials tried to play down the illicit origins of the conflict, opponents gave it a name that made the link quite clear: the Opium War.

The first Opium War had begun and British forces, directed by Foreign Secretary Lord Palmerston, sent a military expedition to Canton demanding reparations for the insult to British honour and the £2 million loss of property in opium chests. British troops slaughtered civilians up and down China's coast. A sense of shame and abhorrence runs through many of the accounts left by British officers in the war. In his journal, one officer confesses, 'Many most barbarous things occurred disgraceful to our men,' while another describes his revulsion at a 'sea blackened with floating corpses'. As the toll of Chinese, Indian and British casualties increased daily and the war languished on, critics were not silent, comparing the opium trade to the recently banned slave trade.

Questions about the legitimacy of the justifications for the war raged. While the British denied any connection to opium and argued that the war was entirely about defending Britain's national honour and protecting their countrymen from alleged atrocities in China, the involvement of opium was inescapable. The name 'Opium War', as the *London Times* and other papers labelled it was an apt yet difficult to digest concept. The notion of going to war to advance the interests of drug dealers was incomprehensible. As William Gladstone wrote in his diary at the time, 'I am in dread of the judgments of God upon England for our national iniquity towards China.'

The British public at large did not have much knowledge or awareness of what was happening in Canton until the London newspapers began reporting events, albeit it several months after they occurred. *The Times*

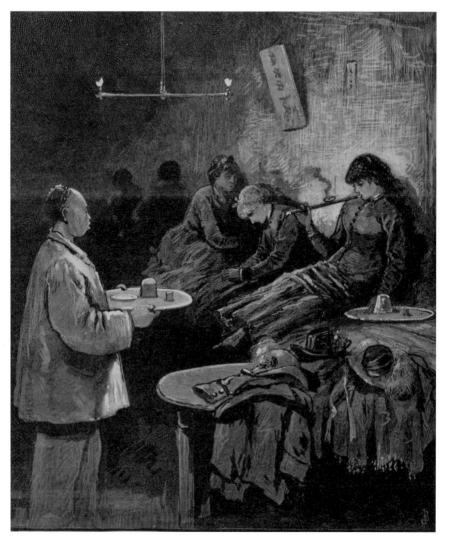

Opium, a growing metropolitan evil. Here's an illustration of an opium den frequented by addicted working girls.

was probably the most influential of the papers due to its widespread readership, having a circulation of 38,100.

British opinion was divided. The opium trade was not generally a topic of great national concern. At the beginning of the war the most important matter seemed to be that the Chinese insulted British dignity and pride by mistreating the expatriate families during the blockade. In this way the war was seen as necessary to defend British honour and national status.

On 7 August 1839, *The Times* reprinted a proclamation from Commissioner Lin, which made an emotional appeal, comparing the great benefits of the tea trade to British citizens to the great harm of opium imports to Chinese consumers, and arguing that British conduct would 'rouse indignation in every human heart, and [was] utterly inexcusable in the eyes of celestial reason.' Despite this, the hearts of the British public remained hardened, with its attention firmly fixed on the maintenance of honour and prestige. *The Times* printed features by some of the leading critics of opium, including an excerpt from Reverend Thelwall's book *Iniquities of the Opium Trade With China*, but the British public was not stirred by the moralistic accounts of opium's destructive effects in China, preferring to believe the overstated reports of the iniquities suffered by their countrymen at the hands of the brutal and vulgar Chinese barbarians.

Perhaps it is not surprising that the British public was not moved by the tales of suffering brought on by opium. Contrary to Lin's belief, opium was not illegal in Britain and was commonly prescribed in many forms, including laudanum; indeed it was seen as no worse than gin or tobacco. However, in the eyes of the British public, Lin had committed an insult and exacted terrible cruelty by blockading and then expelling British compatriots by force, insulting their honour and discrediting them. As more sensational accounts of the blockade were featured, *The Times* told of 'intimidation' tactics, that were 'threatening the lives of the Hong merchants'. The readers were appalled to read of the subsequent forced expulsion of British families from Macao, and British anger rose further at the perceived insult to British dignity. Many readers might have echoed Samuel Warren's sentiments in 'The Opium Question': 'In the name of the dear glory and honour of old England, where are the councils which will hesitate for a moment in cleansing them, even if it be in blood, from the stains which barbarian insolence has so deeply tarnished them? Why are there not seen and heard there, by those incredulous and vaunting barbarians, the glare and thunder of our artillery?' Many members of the British public felt that merchants could not be held accountable for the moral rights and wrongs of dealing opium when the British government explicitly condoned the Company's activities. The fact was that members of the British Parliament, the East India Company, and British merchants who traded opium in Chinese ports were all complicit in the sale of an addictive substance and in defiance of the Qing's efforts to stop it, therefore China's treatment of our British merchants was unjust.

The war continued and debate in Parliament focused on the central themes of protecting opium production in India and defending British profits made from that revenue source. The Opposition focused its attacks on the government's clumsy handling of Chinese officials and allowing misunderstandings to get this far, but even they were not opposed to fighting the war itself. Indeed, even William Gladstone, who had openly denounced the moral vicissitudes of the opium trade, stopped short of demanding that the military operations in India come to a halt. Though his disdain for the contraband imports into China were clear, 'Does the Minister not know that the opium smuggled into China comes exclusively from British ports, that it is from Bengal and through Bombay? [...] we require no preventive service to put down this illegal traffic. We have only to stop the sailings of the smuggling vessels.'

However thinly masked the imperial motives were, they were shared by a majority of the British Parliament, but as the war dragged on criticisms began to creep in over the length of time the opium matter was taking to resolve. Even the press support began to wane. In April 1841 *The Times* ran a satirical letter from an imaginary Chinese opium addict, thanking the British Royal Naval Officer, Charles Elliot for rescuing him from Lin Zexu. In this satirical account the opium addict describes how he had been arrested, his opium and smoking paraphernalia confiscated and his salvation had come in the form of the British fleet. He was released, 'bought opium of thy soldiers', and was 'given back to liberty'.

The Times joined many of the war's former opponents and formulated an attack on the Whig leadership for allowing the war to drag on. Nearly two years after the war had started the Whig government toppled through a successful vote of no confidence that was unrelated to China. The Conservative opposition formed a new government. Recognising that they needed to end the war quickly, the new government mobilised more British forces in China and took the stance that, as there was no hope of reconciliation, victory was now the only solution.

In August 1842, China lost the war. She was forced to open up five ports to the British and had to limit tariffs and grant rights for the British in China. The Opium War destroyed the Chinese government's legitimacy, allowing the British to make demands as they pleased. Victory spelled great commercial benefit for Britain while the Chinese bore the weight of all war reparations, which dealt a devastating blow to her economy.

COMMERCE ANGLAIS.

La Caricature

Grandville inv.   Imp d'Aubert & C.º   Forest lith

Yé vo dis qu'il faut, qué vo ach'té ce poisonne to d'suite, no vollons qué vo empposonniéz vo vériléblement, pou quéno avions du thé bocoupe pou digerer confortéblement nos Berfteakes!

The Opium War. Here we have a satirical illustration showing an Englishman ordering the emperor of China to buy opium. Another Chinese man lies dead on the floor with troops in the background, one man is poised to fire a gun. The text says: "I tell you to immediately buy the gift here. We want you to poison yourself completely, because we need a lot of tea in order to digest our beefsteaks."

Fourteen years later there was a Second Opium War, which lasted from 1856 to 1860. China lost again and was this time dealt the penalty of having to legalise opium. William Gladstone, who came from the same Liberal Party as Palmerston, became prime minister in 1865. Gladstone had been a staunch critic of Britain's involvement in the opium trade and lambasted the two Opium Wars as 'Palmerston's war', but even he recognised that the lucrative opium trade was too valuable to prohibit.

The legalisation of opium led to the massive domestic production of the drug and the role of opium as Britain's cash cow was now set to end. By 1906 the importance of opium in the West's trade with China had declined to an insignificant level, while China turned itself into the prime producer in order to satisfy the rapidly growing demand from its addicted nation. Heroin and morphine, addictive drugs manufactured directly from opium, spread to the rest of the world quickly because of the huge quantity of opium being produced, and the opium trade became a global problem as early as the turn of the nineteenth century.

Opium was a growing concern in England. The topic of addiction raged and the scales of public opinion tipped between seeing the addicted as morally bankrupt criminals or victims of circumstance. Public opinion about the opium epidemic was strongly influenced by professional, social, political and international interests.

Class and racial tensions contributed to the mounting public concern. Whilst opium was considered 'respectable' for the middle class to use, its spread to the working classes caused concerns about opium abuse contributing to social decay. Later, public sentiment and racial intolerance were stirred up as opium became associated with Chinese opium dens; in particular, young white women were thought to be at risk of being corrupted by foreigners.

Early medical discussions during this time had little to do with opium's addictive potential. Instead, doctors and medical experts had addressed opium's role in limiting life expectancy and in accidental poisoning, as well as the lack of product purity in the market. As early as 1840 Dr Anthony Todd Thomson, at a meeting of the Westminster Medical Society, told his colleagues that he 'had no doubt that consuming opium, either in the crude or liquid state, or inhaling it from a pipe, tended materially to shorten life.' However, no mention of the effects of addiction was made. Amidst mounting pressure from public opinion, racial tensions and international pressures, the focus was still not upon the issue of opium addiction, but on how to restrict self-medication and regulate where opium was sold. Pharmacists spotted an opportunity to monopolise the lucrative opiate trade and advocated for the 1868 Pharmacy Act, which limited opium's point of sale to pharmacists. On 31 July 1868 the

Chinese opium - An illustration showing the negative and destructive nature of the opium business.

Pharmacy Act was passed in Britain. This was the country's first piece of legislation to restrict the sale of poisons to qualified persons.

International political and economic pressures also played an important role. The 1874 Society for the Suppression of the Opium Trade was created specifically to campaign against Britain's involvement in the opium trade with China. It had become a forceful voice in describing opium's addictive nature. Public concern was mounting and in the 1860s the British press and popular literature campaigned to restrict usage, printing sensationalist artwork and poetry highlighting the destructive nature of opium dens.

Within a century, societal and cultural factors shaped an evolving public perception of opiates. At the beginning of the nineteenth century it was considered innocuous enough for babies, but by the end it was viewed as an immoral, addictive drug to be tightly regulated. As the negative effects of laudanum became better-documented – the euphoria it provided was followed by crashing lows, restlessness, torpor, and sweats – it became clear that the drug needed to be better regulated. The mainstream view of opiates contained within potions and tonics was not easily changed, though accounts by addicts helped to sway

An opium den in the east end of London.

public opinion. In 1889 the *Journal of Mental Sciences* published an emotive account from a former drug-addicted girl:

> My principal feeling was one of awful weariness and numbness at the end of my back; it kept me tossing about all day and night long. It was impossible to lie in one position for more than a minute, and of course sleep was out of the question. I was so irritable that no one cared to come near me; mother slept on the sofa in my room, and I nearly kicked her once for suggesting that I should say hymns over to myself, to try and make me go to sleep. Hymns of a very different sort were in my mind. I was once or twice very nearly strangling myself, and I am ashamed to say that the only thing that kept me from doing so was the thought that I would be able to get laudanum somehow. I was conscious of feeling nothing but the mere sense of being alive, and if the house had been burning, would have thought it too much of an effort to rise.

Opium addiction was not just a concern in China and England, but in America as well, as this depiction of a New York opium den illustrates.

Accounts such as these, accompanied by growing medical reports highlighting the dangers of opiates and the rising death toll for adults and children as a direct result of their use, eventually spelled out the dangers to the British public.

Despite all the issues surrounding opium and the direct link between the import of tea and this 'immoral drug', the popularity of tea never waned. Trade with China had brought widespread familiarity with tea as well as other foreign goods, so much so that tea was now an everyday commodity and had become a necessity in British life. The Opium Wars did not halt British trade with China. In fact, after the Treaty of Nanking, which marked the end of the First Opium War, trade increased. However, the unsettled relationship with China meant that the British were forced to begin securing a tea supply from elsewhere. From 1839 to 1842 the new British tea industry in Assam was just beginning to bud and by 1852 the British tea industry was on its way to becoming a flourishing success.

Chapter 4

Tea Addiction, Smuggling, Swindles and Taxation

Britain had developed a taste for tea and as the middle classes slurped, sipped and savoured the brew, the taxes and trade monopoly kept the prices high.

Eighteenth-century Britain was coloured by the phenomenal increase in the number and weightiness of taxes: from the Revolution to the defeat of Napoleon, tax revenues leapt from around £2 million to nearly £80 million. Despite these huge tax hikes the government did not have a limitless ability to collect taxes, for in addition to the popular public opposition to taxes on everyday commodities such as tobacco, wine, ale and cider, the government's ability to levy tax was also hampered by fraud and smuggling, thus limiting their ability to enforce the payment of duties levied, and the amount of tax that a particular commodity could yield.

Any romantic notions of smuggling that consist of images of boats moored in lonely coves at night, while the crew hurriedly unload its cargo of tea in the moonlight, or of men expectantly waiting with pack horses while lookouts stand guard against a surprise seizure by customs officers are rather quixotic. These events were romanticised in Kipling's 'A Smugglers Song':

Five and twenty ponies
Trotting through the dark,
Brandy for the Parson
Baccy for the clerk.

The reality of smuggling, however, was far removed from Kipling's verse. It was often gruesome, and just another element that added to the blood-soaked history of tea. An account of smuggling in

A smuggler depicted in a variety of situations and positions.

Strand Magazine on 5 March 1891 tells a tale of unlawful death and villainy: 'The evasion of custom duties has since custom duties were first collected by Government been in this country almost a national vice and the criminal records contain many horrible stories of savagely murdered customs officers, whose lives went in the execution of their duties.'

There is no doubt that smuggling could be a savage business. It was a trade triggered by increasingly high tariffs or duties, which a merchant would have to pay to legally import tea. And when the import duties reached a staggering 119 per cent in the 1750s, it made the risks involved in smuggling worthwhile: after all, if you could avoid paying the tax, the cost of your daily brew dropped by more than half. The risks were high but the potential rewards alluring, a combination that meant smuggled consignments were worth protecting at any cost.

In the 1770s the cost of living rose as the country's national debt spiralled, after having waged an expensive and ultimately futile military campaign to retain control of the colonies. As the country faced financial crisis, taxes rapidly rose in an attempt to steer it away from bankruptcy.

The tax on tea hit 110 per cent, while brandy and gin attracted more than eighteen different duties totaling 250 per cent and the tax on tobacco made up more than ninety-five per cent of its retail price. It wasn't just luxury items that were taxed steeply. By the late eighteenth century salt was inflated to forty times its original price. This caused serious issues for fishermen who relied on salt to preserve their catches. The hike in price made the purchase of salt impossible and fishing communities faced financial ruin. But these heavily taxed products were all available for a fraction of the price from nearby France and the Channel Islands; smuggling was set to become a thriving industry.

There are two distinct schools of thought when it comes to the justification of smuggling goods. Samuel Johnson described the smuggler as 'a wretch who, in defiance of justice and the laws, imports or exports goods either contraband or without payment of the customs.' Adam Smith, the eighteenth-century economist and advocate of free trade, was more generous, describing the smuggler as 'a person who, though no doubt blameable for violating the laws of his country, is frequently incapable of violating those of natural justice, and would have been in every respect an excellent citizen had not the laws of his country made that a crime which nature never meant to be so.'

Whatever the morality of the trade, by its very nature smuggling attracted some of the worst characters in society. A market for cheap goods and the prospect of financial gain was a magnet for recruiting hoodlums and villains into the smuggler fold. Brandy, tobacco and tea proved to be popular goods on an increasingly popular black market. Both the government and the East India Company were increasingly concerned about the problem of smuggling and the loss of revenue it caused. They calculated that three million pounds of tea a year had been smuggled during the first half of the eighteenth century, three times the amount of legal sales. Later, in 1779, in response to estimates of seven million pounds of tea lost each year, Parliament passed another act against smuggling in an attempt to clamp down on the contraband barons that were turning the cliffs of the British coastline into a gangster's paradise.

Brutality and violence were often central themes in smuggling. The presence of ruthless villains and the promise of profits led to violent clashes between rival smuggling groups and revenue officers, and led to some stomach-churning crimes.

An early example of the ferocity and violence of smugglers is seen in the actions of the infamous Hawkhurst Gang who operated on the south coast of England in the mid-eighteenth century. This gang committed two vile murders to protect their smuggling interests and at the heart of the crime lay a small packet of tea. On the night of 22 September 1747, customs officers intercepted a smuggler's boat off the coast of Dorset and, after confiscating its haul of rum, brandy and two tons of tea wrapped in oilskin, the contraband was impounded in the king's Custom House at Poole.

The smugglers refused to be thwarted and have valuable cargo confiscated. Sixty members of the gang took part in a raid on the Customs House to retrieve their smuggled tea, leaving the cumbersome barrels of booze behind. Having retrieved the tea, they rode north through the small Hampshire town of Fordingbridge in a show of fearless bravado, making no attempt to disguise themselves or their actions. One of the smugglers, John Diamond, recognised one of the villagers, Daniel Chater, having briefly worked with him, and gave Chater a small bag of tea.

The Hawkhurst gang had operated freely through threats of violence and intimidation, frightening local people into keeping quiet and burning down the property of any local magistrates who attempted to interfere with their activities. But the attack on the Customs House showed such flagrant disregard for the authorities that the powers-that-be were forced to try and take action and began to make enquiries.

Unfortunately for Daniel Chater, the gift of tea was a poison chalice. It wasn't long until the customs officials heard that he knew the identity of one of the smugglers and he was pressurised into agreeing to give evidence against John Diamond. On 14 February 1748 Chater and a customs officer named William Galley set out to ride to Chichester to see a magistrate. On the way they stopped at the White Hart pub in Rowlands Castle.

The landlady of the White Hart had two sons who were smugglers, and she became increasingly suspicious of her guests, sending word to her sons and their smuggling colleagues. Members of the Hawkhurst Gang arrived at the White Hart and proceeded to get Chater and Galley drunk. While the pair were in a drunken stupor their bags were rifled and evidence of their identities and intentions against the gang revealed.

The gang horsewhipped the pair and then tied them to horses for the fifteen-mile ride to another village. Weak from the constant whipping, the two men frequently slid from the saddles and hung beneath their horses' bellies so that the hooves struck their heads. Galley begged to be killed quickly, but the smugglers showed no mercy and continued whipping and beating them.

By the time they arrived at their destination, the Red Lion at Rake, Galley was in a bad way and after a final flogging he appeared to be dead. They buried his body in a foxhole and turned their attentions to Chater. They starved and tortured him for two days and then, upon deciding that simply shooting him was too lenient, took him to a well. As he knelt to pray, one of the gang slashed his face with such brutality that his nose was cut off and his eye was severely damaged. In a bid to end his life quickly, Chater attempted to jump down the well, but he was stopped and the gang suspended him in a noose over the well. After surviving the botched hanging, the smugglers cut him down and hurled him down the well head first. He could still be heard groaning at the bottom so the gang threw rocks and debris into the well until Chater's cries ceased.

The gang became concerned that their possession of Galley and Chater's horses would be incriminating, so they butchered Galley's horse (they could not find Chater's). Having successfully run a racket of intimidation and violence, the group was confident that they would get away with their crimes, but substantial rewards were offered for their arrest and when one gang member gave evidence against the others in return for leniency the grisly details of the two murders were finally uncovered.

The whereabouts of the bodies were revealed and it was only when the authorities went to recover them that they realised the full horror of the crimes the Hawkhurst Gang had committed. When Chater was brought up from the well, one of his legs had been entirely severed by the horrific injuries inflicted upon him, but it was Galley's body that caused the most shock. He was found in an upright position, with his hands in front of eyes: it was clear that he had been buried alive.

There was outcry at the brutality of these crimes and the public silence was broken. Eight of the ringleaders were tried and sentenced to death. One of them died before he could be executed, but his dead body was still put in chains and hung in the open air as a warning for all. While the murders of Galley and Chater were especially barbaric, they were by no means isolated incidents. A few months after, two members of the Hawkhurst Gang who had not yet been arrested accused a farm labourer of stealing two small bags of tea from a large stash of smuggled tea that

Galley Grove, Rogate, West Sussex. The grove is named after William Galley, a customs officer who was tortured and murdered by the Hawkhurst Gang in 1748 and buried, possibly whilst still alive, in a foxhole in the grove.

they had concealed in a barn where he was working. Though the labourer denied taking the tea and begged them to spare him on account of his wife and children, they whipped him to death and then threw his body, weighted down with rocks, into a pond. Later, they returned to the barn and discovered the missing bags of tea, which they had simply misplaced.

It wasn't just the Hawkshurst Gang that were violent; there are multiple accounts of murders and brutal attacks at the hands of smuggling gangs. Despite the brutality, tea drinking had become such a national addiction that many people continued to turn a blind eye to the activities of the smuggling gangs and the blood being shed in the name of affordable tea. By the 1780s smuggling was so prolific that an anonymous author wrote about fears for decency and order as thousands of men had turned away from respectable jobs in order to be employed in the lucrative smuggling trade: 'Thousands who would otherwise be employed in fishing, agriculture etc., to the emolument of this kingdom are now supported in drunkenness, rioting, and debauchery by their iniquitous traffic; a traffic obviously productive of so numerous a train of evils, that prudence, common honesty, decency, order, and civil government, unitedly cry out for redress.'

With the price and demand for tea both sky high, smuggling was showing no signs of decline. Through time it even became more sophisticated, more organised and more ruthless. Smugglers were starting to resemble criminal barons rather than small-scale contraband importers. Smuggling was able to thrive partly because of the peaceable conditions in Europe from the mid-1760s, which encouraged more European trade with China, and which in turn meant more tea imported to the continent that could then be smuggled to Britain. Gangs crewed large, heavily armed ships, which carried hundreds of chests of tea and gallons of spirits like rum and brandy. Distribution was carried out through highly organised networks that transported the smuggled tea far inland.

"Loading a Smuggler", a caricature.

The distribution of smuggled tea in London was, in fact, as organised as that of legal tea, and the smugglers' ships could even be insured against loss or seizure at Lloyd's of London. The organisation of the contraband tea made it no less aggressive, though; the world of smuggling was still dominated by hardened crooks with a mind for violence.

Smugglers were always devising new methods to stop their swag being discovered. Women were often used, not just as messengers and signalers, but also to carry contraband from the shores, as their attire was well suited to the surreptitious secretion of all manner of smuggled goods: 18lb of tea could be hidden under the cape or petticoat trouser worn by the fishermen and vessel crew, while cotton bags made into the shape of the crown of a hat, a cotton waistcoat, and a cotton bustle and thigh pieces combined could hold 30lb of tea. A report from the *Hampshire Chronicle* of 25 March 1799 stated that:

> A woman of the name of Maclane, residing at Gosport, accustomed to supply the crew of Queen Charlotte with slops went out in a wherry to Spithead, when a sudden squall coming on, the boat sank; the watermen were drowned, but the life of the woman was providentially saved, by being buoyed up with a quantity of bladders, which had been secreted round her for the purpose of smuggling liquor into the ship, until she was picked up by the boat of a transport lying near.

Smugglers had even refined the art of illusion in order to hide their illegally imported goods. Tea cases were fitted between the vessel's timbers and were made to resemble the floors of the ship.

The extent of smuggling in eighteenth-century Britain is by its very nature an elusive topic. Smuggling was enough of a problem to prompt the government to conduct three official inquiries in half a century. Between 1689 and 1784 sixty-three acts of Parliament were passed that were linked or concerned with countering tax-dodging practices that defrauded them of revenue, notwithstanding the thirty-nine failed attempts to pass such legislation in the same period.

Both the 1746 and 1783 inquiries highlighted tea as being the staple commodity of smuggling. Tea was a favourite with smugglers because of its compact nature, unlike clumsy spirit barrels. The first report from the latter inquiry estimated that thirteen million pounds of tea was consumed in the country each year, more than double the six million imported by the East India Company. Reports from both inquiries argued that tackling the smuggling of tea would remove the support to the rest of the illicit trade.

The Commutation Act of 1784 sought to address this issue by transferring the legal incidence of part of the duty on tea from the merchant to the consumer through an addition to the window tax (a property tax based on the number of windows in a house). The exorbitant taxes had done little to curb the British appetite for tea. By 1784 all social and economic classes in Britain were drinking tea on a regular basis and tea-gardens were at the height of their popularity. Although the tax had no bearing on how much tea the British consumed, it certainly had an impact on how people got their hands on it.

Smuggling evolved as a way to circumvent some of the worst of the taxes levied on legally imported tea, and was so rife that even some members of the East India Trading Company's own crew were smuggling tea in to sell illegally in Britain. Parliament tried to restrain the smuggling before 1784, but was unsuccessful. The newly formed Smuggling Committee of 1745 called in many witnesses to ascertain the extent and causes of smuggling, as well as to discuss preventative measures, but the general consensus was that smuggling was profitable, avoided high taxes, brought in exotic commodities, and was even considered a legitimate part of local economies. Parliament chose to ignore the advice of the committee in regard to high taxes for fear of damage to a primary source of Britain's income and instead focus upon stiffer penalties for smuggling offences.

Smugglers were mainly a home-grown problem. There was the odd foreign smuggler, but most were natives. Mr Samuel Wilson, grocer and former runner of contraband goods, testified at the Smuggling Committee of 1745 that 'the vessels employed in the running of goods do most of them belong to the subjects of this Kingdom, and are generally Folkstone cutters that the smugglers buy their goods with money, or wool; and that the principal commodity is tea.'

Parliament was eventually forced to act on the matter after the committee's witnesses estimated that almost three million pounds of tea were being smuggled into Britain every year, almost three times that of legal imports.

An oil painting of smugglers by George Morland.

Parliament temporarily cut taxes in the Commutation Act of 1745 in an attempt to help the East India Company overcome the issue of competing against illegal imports and thus protect its revenue stream. By 1784 the situation had not improved. The Company's profits were still being undermined by illegal imports, so Parliament was obliged to pass another Commutation Act, this time one that lowered the tax on tea to just 12 ½ per cent. This huge tax cut spelled an end to many smuggling operations as there was no need to evade the Company's prices with tea becoming more affordable than ever before, but it wouldn't silence the critics of the East India Company for long.

The Commutation Act benefited not only the tea-drinking public and the East India Company, but also the small merchants who could now expand their sales as they were able to afford to carry more stock. Grocers were the primary sellers of tea outside coffee-houses and tea-gardens, and sold tea to a vast array of customers, often competing for custom on the basis of price. Tax cuts meant the possibility of increased sales and more flexibility in scaling prices. Grocers were an important link in the distribution of tea to the public, not just because they sold it, but because they also mixed their own tea blends for the convenience of

Tea-Time by Jan Josef Horemans II (1714-1790).

their customers. The art of blending teas was beginning to refine the British palate, making consumers aware of more sophisticated blends of their favorite drink and encouraging them to develop a blend allegiance rather than just a straightforward preference for a particular tea leaf. Blended teas would, however, soon become another avenue of exploitation.

By the mid-eighteenth century tea had became the country's most popular drink and had pushed ale and gin from their place in British hearts. With the slashed tea taxes, smuggling became pointless and virtually all tea was imported legally by the East India Company. However, the Company's woes were not over. Tea smuggling had hit its profits hard and it was struggling to recover. Moreover, it still had to contend with the issue of adulteration.

The adulteration of tea was a major problem. Tea was commonly bulked out with everything from twigs and sawdust to iron filings, and while these additions were unpleasant, they were not as toxic as some of the colourants employed in adulteration practices. A concoction of various organic and artificial additives were routinely added to tea leaves before sale.

It was not just straightforward adulteration of tea leaves that was the problem, it was also the production of counterfeit tea, called 'smouch', sometimes referred to as 'English Tea'. Smouch was widely available and presented a real problem. Imitation green tea would contain a variety of leaves such as ash and hawthorn, and would be dyed with green vitriol or vedigris. Imitation black tea often contained hawthorn, ash and sloe leaves combined with chamber lye (the contents of the chamber pot) or animal dung and bran. Once ground down it was said that such a mixture strongly resembled the popular Bohea tea.

In an act passed by the British government in 1725 such blends were condemned:

> Very great quantities of sloe leaves, liquorice leaves, and the leaves of tea that have been before used, or the leaves of other trees, shrubs or plants in imitation of tea […] and do likewise mix, colour, stain and dye such leaves, and likewise tea with terra japonica, sugar, molasses, clay, logwood and other ingredients, and do sell and vend the same as true and real tea, to the prejudice of the health of His Majesty's subjects, the diminution of the revenue and to the ruin of the fair trader.

It is certain that the practice of making smouch was common and some have estimated that around three million pounds in weight were produced every year. Jonas Hanway, writing in 1756, confirmed the trade in used leaves: 'You have also heard, that your maids sometimes dry your leaves and sell them: the industrious nymph who is bent on gain may get a shilling a pound for such tea. These leaves are dyed in solution of Japan earth'.

The practice of producing smouch was not just a problem for consumers, but also for honest merchants. In 1785 Richard Twining wrote a graphic account of tea adulteration in the pamphlet *Observations on the Tea & Window Act and on the Tea Trade*:

> I shall here communicate to the Public a particular account of this manufacture, which I have lately received from a gentleman, who has made very accurate enquiries on the subject.

METHOD OF MAKING SMOUCH WITH ASH LEAVES TO MIX WITH BLACK TEAS

When gathered they are first dried in the sun then baked. They are next put on the floor and trod upon until the leaves are small, then lifted and steeped in copperas, with sheep's dung, after which, being dried on the floor, they are fit for use.

Twining suggested that in one small part of England, approximately twenty tons of smouch were manufactured every year. No doubt Twining bolstered his own trade by highlighting the practices of unscrupulous tea traders.

While green tea was the initial style of tea introduced and originally enjoyed in Britain, it was falling out of fashion quickly due to a growing number of concerns circulating about its safety. Some of these concerns were unfounded notions of hysteria and insomnia, but there were also genuine worries about it being toxic as a result of widespread adulteration. Green tea was generally thought to be easier to adulterate and so wary consumers were anxious about its purity.

There was a commercial benefit to green tea falling out of favour, for while both black and green teas are made from the leaves of the same plant, black tea is oxidized and therefore is drier and more compact than the wetter green tea. This made it better suited to long-haul journeys in terms of lower spoilage risks, and being drier it was suitable for compressing and compacting, thus saving space on board ships and in turn increasing profits. Therefore, any concerns about green tea would be commercially exploited wherever possible. Tea adulteration became so prolific that green tea was soon considered far more of a health risk than opium.

Adulteration did not come in just one guise. Devious businessmen with their eye on profit both in Canton and England resorted to all kinds of unseemly practices to bulk out consignments of green tea. It was

Different types of tea.

not just cut with other leaves to bulk it out, but dyed with highly toxic copper carbonate and lead chromate to enhance its green appearance. So common was this practice that when retailers attempted to sell pure, uncoloured green tea it was considered to be the wrong colour.

In 1839 the British medical journal *The Lancet* featured a paper by Dr George Sigmond on the effects of tea on health. Sigmond concluded that while green tea did carry medicinal properties, being warming and comforting and much better than fermented liquors, he advised against excessive intake. Some of those partial to partaking in green tea, he wrote, would complain 'of a sensation of sinking at the stomach, a craving, an emptiness, and a fluttering in the chest.' To soothe these 'miserable sensations', he continued, these green-tea drinkers become dependent on drinking a glass of brandy an hour after tea.

The paper cited a case from the *Glasgow Medical Journal* where a woman was 'attacked with excruciating pain at the stomach,' and 'distressing symptoms of hysteria uttering dreadful shrieks and perspiring profusely from the forehead.' Her symptoms were ascribed to her daily morning ritual of drinking strong green tea on an empty stomach, without the dilution of milk, cream or sugar. Her symptoms were described as only being alleviated by 'the enormous dose of six grains of solid opium and four drachmas of tincture.'

Green tea had become the villain of the Victorian age, but the reality was that unscrupulous merchants also stretched black tea supplies by defiling it with a number of added extras, including black lead and floor sweepings. Dishonest dealers added everything and anything to both green and black tea, including iron filings and the leaves of other plants such as ash or hawthorn. Even more worrying was their practice of dying tea leaves with toxic verdigris, Prussian blue, Dutch pink, ferrous sulphate, copper carbonate and even cutting the tea with sheep dung.

Tea adulteration was so commonplace that people believed the artificial colours achieved through the introduction of additives to be natural. Indeed, people expected green tea to have a slight blue hue to it. Robert Fortune explained in *A Journey to the Tea Countries of China* (1852) that the long-established method of the Chinese had been to 'crush Prussian Blue to a fine powder and add gypsum in a ration of three to four resulting in a light blue dye powder. Add the powder five minutes before the end of the last roasting.' A London newspaper called the *Family Herald* commented on Fortune's publication, observing, 'We

Englishmen swallow tea, go to bed, turn and toss, keep awake, get up, complain of unstrung nerves and weak digestion, and visit the doctor, who shakes his head and says, "tea!" This is what he says, but what he means is "Metallic paint".'

Counterfeit tea was near impossible to detect once it had been added to a tea blended by a knowledgeable and skilled, if somewhat dishonest, tea merchant. However, it was blatantly obvious when added to unblended tea leaves. So many discerning tea-drinkers made it a point to only purchase unblended teas, though these were far more expensive. In the homes of the privileged and wealthy it became customary for the lady of the house to blend the tea to be served to her guests herself. That way guests would be assured that they would be getting an unadulterated tea.

In a work entitled *Tsiology; A discourse on Tea* (1827) a tea dealer wrote that such was the public fear about adulterated tea that a dealer was regarded 'almost as a secret assassin, ready to enter every man's house to poison him and his family. It almost converted the English into a nation of botanists'. The tea dealer went on to explain that 'Every man endeavoured to detect the lurking poison, and suspected death in the pot.'

The government was not keen to act on this adulteration. Indeed, they expressed disbelief and denied that food adulteration was a widespread epidemic, making vague suggestions that it would all be sorted out by market forces. *The Lancet* was key in launching a campaign to illustrate just how widespread the issue was, using the work of Dr Arthur Hill Hassall and publishing his reports to illustrate the problem of food and drink adulteration. His reports were predictably unpopular with food producers and some retailers, but they were instrumental in lobbying change. In the 1850s Hassell carried out an analysis of various London foods and found that there was not a single loaf of bread that tested alum-free, and that a long list of ingredients, including tea, mustard, pickles, beer and milk, which may have been perceived pure by consumers, were tested as potentially deadly. Eventually the government passed the Food Adulteration Act (1860), which was a step in the right direction but fell short of solving the adulteration problem.

As the battle for a decent act of Parliament continued, buying food remained a deathly game of roulette. Contamination from rodents, insects and faecal contagion was common in many foodstuffs, and caused diphtheria, scarlet fever, diarrhoea, and enteric fever as well as other long- and short-term illnesses.

While tea imported from China was reported to contain sand, dirt and traces of sulphate of iron, shopkeepers and traders also employed adulteration and other sharp practices, meaning that food often fell nutritionally short or contained dangerous additives. From strychnine and cocculus inculus added to rum and beer, to lead added to mustard, snuff and cider, you could never be sure when your last meal would come.

So many toxic additives were used, regularly and extensively, that they had a cumulative effect, resulting in chronic gastritis and often fatal food poisoning. And though people steered clear of green tea for fear of poisoning, the new trend for black tea led to the addition of milk and sugar being more common, thus adding to the risk factor of tea drinking. Sugar had been revealed to contain ground glass while milk was watered down and chalk added to make it look more wholesome. Luxury milk-based products such as ice cream were a cocktail of foreign bodies: samples of ice cream taken by the London County Medical Officer revealed cocci, bacilli, torulae, cotton fiber, lice, bed bugs, bug's legs, fleas, straw, human hair, and cat and dog hair.

The addition of milk in tea was of particular concern. In 1882, 20,000 milk samples were tested and the results showed that a fifth had been adulterated, much of it happening in the home. Many householders did not have the luxury of the fresh milk we are accustomed to today. Boracic acid was believed to purify milk, removing the sour taste and smell from milk that had spoiled. Mrs Beeton advised that this was 'quite a harmless addition', but in reality even small amounts of boracic acid can cause nausea, vomiting, abdominal pain and diarrhoea. A more sinister problem, however, came from bovine TB. Before the practice of pasturisation was introduced, milk very often contained bovine TB, which flourished in its bacteria-rich environment. In humans this leads to damage of the internal organs, spinal bone damage and deformity. It is estimated that around half a million children died from bovine tuberculosis contracted from milk during the Victorian period. Brewing tea and adding milk to it could be extremely dangerous.

Adulteration of tea wasn't the only way that a consumer could be ripped off in pursuit of their supplies. Used tea leaves were plentiful and for those women in the fortunate position of working as a housekeeper or cook in affluent households, their entitlement to the used leaves would form part of the contract and made for a welcome and profitable perk. Such women would dry and sell the used leaves to a char woman

"I DRINK TO THE GENERAL DEATH OF THE WHOLE TABLE."

This cartoon was awarded first prize by the American Medical Association.

A drawing depicting the dangers of impure milk, taken from a book written by Nathan Straus on the pasteurisation of milk.

or directly to less fortunate families for as much as a shilling a pound. The char woman might take the leaves and sell them on to a slop shop, who would then process them for resale. Old leaves would be stiffened with a gum solution, coloured with either black lead or iron sulphate and combined with some fresh leaves. If the slop shop wanted to bulk out the old leaves they would do so with the addition of willow, sloe leaves and floor sweepings. At least this mixture contained some tea, albeit it low grade, and would have imparted a tea flavour and aroma.

For those Victorians who managed to survive food adulteration and contamination, help was at hand in the shape of the 1875 Sale of Food and Drinks Act, which had powers to appropriately tackle food adulteration (this act still forms the basis of current legislation today). The legislation was effective and by the 1880s, not only were foods generally testing negative for adulterants, but more forward-thinking companies were realising that there was more profit to be made from food marketed as wholesome and pure. The end of loose products such as tea, coffee and cocoa was in sight and the era of such products being sold in sealed, hygienic packets with a clear maker's mark as a brand of quality was on the horizon.

Chapter 5

Tea and Seduction

When we think about seduction, many images are conjured. We might see a woman with locks flowing free, her doe-eyes fluttering. We may think of all the sensory details associated with seduction, such as touch, smell, taste and sound. Or perhaps we might consider tea, offered by the English to seduce a whole nation into addiction.

From the late eighteenth century onwards, tea and seduction became synonymous. Many popular plays of the time including *Take Tea in the Arbor* (1840), *A Mistress and her Servant* (1870), and *A Storm in a Tea Cup* (1854) all cited the social importance of taking tea. Increasingly, such plays hinted at the possibility of sexual tension and playfulness.

Five O'Clock Tea by Julius Leblanc Stewart, 1883-4, oil on canvas.

In *Five o'clock Tea* (1854), flirtation and courtship are played out when a young woman invites a number of people for tea that afternoon. The first to arrive is a young gentleman who has a romantic interest in her. He is pleasantly surprised to be the first to arrive. Hostess and guest snatch a few private moments together, during which they indulge in some personal chit-chat.

While the eighteenth-century leisure gardens offered tea in curtained cubicles, the rise of taking tea as a sociable activity at home was an opportunity for middle-class sexual play. The ritual of the sociable tea gathering offered women a temporary power, although this was only extended to the wealthy and privileged and was only in effect for a short period of time during the day. Tea gained further erotic undertones with the introduction of the tea gown, an item of clothing that allowed women a certain amount of bodily freedom.

The tea gown offered the period lady a chance to relax, free from the bustles and corsets of the day in the company of her close companions. Inspired by mediaevalist costume in Pre-Raphaelite paintings, tea gowns were romantically seductive. Designed without boning or bustles they were daring for the times. It was inevitable that the garment's relative ease of fastening and connotations of liberation would make these sociable gatherings the natural setting for seduction.

The trend for sociable teas that did not include food emerged. In *Manners of Modern Society* (1875), Cheadle defines the roles of tea with and tea without food, explaining that tea taken with food in the mid-afternoon is a cost-effective way to feed a crowd, whereas tea taken without food in the afternoon is 'sociable tea'.

Cheadle advises that sociable teas require little if any food and are preferably served without staff, with their primary purpose being social engagement, 'People do not assemble at these five o' clock teas to eat and drink, but merely to see and talk to each other, and take a cup of tea as refreshment.'

With the establishment of social tea as a fashionable ritual and the soft, flowing tea gown with its feminine lines and suggestive appeal, it is perhaps not surprising that social tea then transformed into what the French called 'le cinq à sept': the accepted time when a lady could entertain her lover with the wordless permission of her husband. It was an unspoken rule that a lady's husband would not enter the drawing room at that hour (perhaps because he was enjoying extra marital frivolities himself), and with the collusion of inconspicuous maids, the lady of the house would announce herself 'at home' solely for the benefit of her gentleman caller.

Later tea gowns were modelled on Japanese kimono, as Britain became gripped by a strong fascination with the exotic Japanese culture. In fact, part of the success of tea parties could be attributed to some of the fascination with Japanese customs. A detailed account of the Japanese tea ceremony is found in E.S. Morse's *Japanese Homes* (1886).

With its saucy connotations, the tea gown soon became a necessary part of a stylish lady's wardrobe. Combining comfort and style, the gown moved seamlessly into the evening and became a dinner tea gown. This version was lower at the décolletage and made more elaborately with seductively decorative

An example of a tea gown. This one features chenile lace.

A link exists between the Japanese kimono and the British tea gown.

embellishments. In Steele and Gardiner's *The Complete Housekeeper and Cook* (1888), it was suggested that women invest in a warmer and a cooler tea dress for travel, and comments upon the similarity between the dressing gown and the tea gown: 'There is, perhaps, nothing more mysterious in nature than the harsh line of decency and indecency which most ladies draw between a tea-gown and a dressing-gown. Attired in one they will face a crowd with complacency; in the other they will fly from a steward. Yet we suspect that, to the ordinary male comprehension, there is no tangible difference between the two.'

Indeed, resemblance of the tea gown to fancy dressing gowns in terms of the looseness of the gown, with a strikingly similar look to robes made for the boudoir, would have made them quite inviting to their male admirers and lovers.

These tempting gowns were intended to be worn at small, informal affairs hosted at home and were made even more arousing because they were not meant to be worn outside of one's own home. The tea gown was the only item of clothing that a middle-class woman was allowed to wear in public or her own home that did not contain boned supports or restraints.

Attired in her tea-gown made of soft satin, light chiffon or fine silk, trimmed with delicate lace and generally free from the confines of corsetry, the hostess must have been greatly alluring to male guests. The fabric caressed the feminine form and gave the promise of easy undressing. As a result, social teas became a hotbed of sexual tension.

These comfortable gowns afforded such femininity that while fashions changed and hemlines rose and fell, the tea gown, which had appeared in England from 1875, enjoyed popularity into the 1920s. The Edwardian style was already to wear chiffon and lace to titillate the male fancy and the soft, flowing tea gown continued in this mode, making the very most of the feminine form. By the time of the Edwardian era, tea gowns had become a regular part of a woman's wardrobe and were considered suitable to wear outside. Consequently, the sexual overtones vanished as these dresses became part of everyday summer fashion, as did the social connotations of tea drinking as something associated with both eloquence and luxury. But while tea's saucy associations may have faded, its naughty reputation remained, which is why it was referred to as 'scandal water'.

Britain's best known madam, Cynthia Payne, who was nicknamed Madame Cyn, ran a brothel that was likened to a vicar's tea party. From an Edwardian, net-curtained home in suburbia, Cynthia Payne ran the

An illustration from 1900, depicting the pleasing visual effect of the tea gown.

most notorious British brothel. When police raided a sex party at her home in December 1978 they found a queue of fifty-three men in the hall and on the stairs waiting patiently with their luncheon vouchers ready to be exchanged for sexual favours from one of the thirteen prostitutes on the premises.

A sign in Payne's kitchen read, 'My house is clean enough to be healthy ... and dirty enough to be happy.' For £25, Cynthia offered discerning clients, including peers, MPs, clergymen, bank managers and captains of industry, a luncheon voucher buffet, which included tea and conversation, cake and sandwiches, wine, a striptease and sex with one of the girls she employed.

The clientele were all over the age of forty and were reported as being well-dressed gentlemen who knew how to treat ladies. They would stand around sipping tea or something a little stronger while politely waiting their turn.

At the close of the sex parties the girls returned the luncheon vouchers to Payne and received £8 for each sexual chore performed. They customarily finished their day's work with a meal of poached egg on toast and a hot cup of tea.

At her trial Payne was charged with running the 'biggest disorderly house' in British history and sentenced to eighteen months in prison. However, the parties would return upon her release, with a strong brew, pretty china, an ice-laden bath full of bottles of wine and spirits, and plenty of tea-fuelled frivolity.

The connection between tea and sex is certainly nothing new. Bada Hutong, just south of Tiananmen Square, was once the Chinese capital's red-light district from the time of the Ming dynasty (1368-1644) until the communists took over in 1949. In its halcyon days this warren of lanes housed more than 300 brothels and 700 opium dens.

There were brothels to cater for every taste and budget. The prettiest, freshest and youngest girls sang songs, poured tea and entertained men. These women's sexual favours could not be bought immediately; instead, would-be suitors wooed them over time with gifts, while enjoying tea and sensual promise. There were also areas where more experienced, heavily perfumed prostitutes openly sold sex for those who wanted to climax quickly.

With the flood of opium into China instigated by The East India Company, opium smoking was considered public enemy number one.

A luncheon voucher advertisement from March 1958.

Classified as a damaging agent for society, the pleasures of the drug were blamed for diverting men from their most basic obligations and making them become morally deficient. Opium was cited as causing men to abandon work, and even sell their wives and children, while prostitutes were believed to be using opium in order to seduce men and gain custom. The consumption of opium had long been employed in brothels in order to calm desire and prolong sexual relations. But though opium was a long-standing feature in brothels, it is often overlooked that women were sometimes lured into prostitution through opium-inflicted poverty. Sometimes married women worked as prostitutes as a result of an apathetic husband's costly opium habits, and often they entered the sex trade with their husband's full knowledge and consent.

Women who smoked opium were frowned upon and treated more harshly than male smokers. It was believed that smoking opium would cause women to abandon and neglect their motherly and marital duties, or else become sterile. But the real picture of opium smoking was of men who were plummeted into moral decay through opium addiction and the women who exploited the drug: the *yanhua*, the young employees who prepared the pipes for the clients in the opium dens, and the prostitutes who used it for seduction.

The link between tea and seduction is long established. This engraving depicts a woman attempting to entice. The taking of tea and opium was commonplace in the brothels of China.

Following the Second Opium War (1856-60), a new breed of customer began frequenting Bada: foreigners from the nearby Legation Quarter. The sex industry and opium trade boomed and by the turn of the century Bada brimmed nightly with rows of red lanterns lighting the girls looking for trade, and the rickshaws were filled with men looking for titillation while the heady scent of opium filled the air.

As tea continued to flow out of British teapots, so a fog of opium smoke wafted through China, and as the good men and women of Britain delighted in the pleasure of the tea in their cups, they were oblivious to the fact that their polite tea drinking was fuelling the drug and sex trade in China.

Chapter 6

Kill or Cure: The Raging Debate about Tea's Curative Powers

As tea's popularity swelled amongst all ranks of society, so too did the controversy about the apparent evils of excessive tea drinking. In a society awash with gloomy gin houses, where everything from infanticide to prostitution was attributed to alcoholism, another drug existed in liquid form that nurtured an addiction that was considered every bit as dangerous.

At first glance, what could be more innocent or more wholesome than a cup of tea in the afternoon? Nothing much, it would appear. But tea had plenty of critics. John Wesley condemned it for being 'extremely hurtful to persons who have weak nerves', and the *British Medical Journal of 1893 proclaimed* that 'the habit of tea-drinking is becoming more and more thoroughly national in the British Islands.'

The *Journal* observed that the declining cost of tea had encouraged the poor to depend upon the substance as a dietary staple and blamed the increase in tea consumption for the rising levels of chronic dyspepsia across working-class communities.

Tea was fast replacing gin as the blight on moral and physical well-being according to the medical community. Like tea, gin started out as a medicine. It was thought to be a cure for gout and indigestion, but most attractive of all was its cheapness and availability. During the 1730s notices could be seen all over London. The message was short and to the point: 'Drunk for 1 penny, Dead drunk for tuppence, Straw for nothing.'

In 1730 in London alone there were more than 7,000 'dram shops', sometimes referred to as 'gin houses', and around 10 million gallons of gin were being distilled annually in the capital. Gin drinking gathered momentum and its overconsumption became endemic. Gin seemed to be available on every street – it was hawked by barbers, peddlers, grocers and market traders – and its use far exceeded that of wine, other spirits and beer.

Gin became the poor man's drink as it was cheap, and some workers were even given the spirit as part of their wages. Duty paid on gin was 2d a gallon, as opposed to 4s 9d on strong beer, so it's not surprising that gin became the social drug of the time, preying on the weak, the vulnerable and the impoverished. Life for the poor was often a hard struggle for survival and gin offered a welcome release from the stench of decay and despair. Cheaper than bread, gin offered 'salvation' to the desperate, the old, infirm and the young. Not only was it highly addictive, but it was laced with poisons in the guise of flavourings. Gin rendered men impotent and women sterile, and is cited as a reason why the birth rate in London at this time was exceeded by the death rate. Laced with turpentine, lime oil and sulphuric acid, it was a lethal combination and caused blindness, death and even madness.

Bootleggers sold their gut-rot gin under fancy names such as 'Cuckold's Comfort', 'Ladies' Delight' and 'Knock Me Down' and gin gnawed at London's underbelly, sending it into a morbid state of social

The son and daughter of drunkard parents, drinking in a gin shop, surrounded by lowly characters. The caption reads: Neglected by their parents, educated only in the streets and falling into the hands of wretches who live upon the vices of others, they are led to the gin shop, to drink at that fountain which nourishes every species of crime.

and moral decay. It was aptly nicknamed 'Mothers' Ruin', as many women resorted to drinking cheap 'bathtub gin' in order to drown their sorrows. As a result, children were neglected and sometimes daughters were sold into prostitution.

The gin craze saw people doing bizarre things to get their hands on a tipple: a cattle drover sold his eleven-year-old daughter to a trader for a gallon of gin, while a coachman pawned his wife for a quart bottle. Gin gave the promise of warmth, escape and the chance to stave off hunger pangs, but ultimately it led many to the debtors' prison or the gallows, or else drove them to madness, suicide and death.

Shocking tales of gin-fuelled crimes and moral transgressions increased. Take the case of William Burroughs, who was charged with assault and robbery in 1731. The court heard of how gin was at the centre of his moral decay: 'He drove Hackney coaches, and by that means fell into that dreadful Society of Gin-drinkers, Whores, Thieves, House-breakers, Street-robbers, Pick-pockets, and the whole train of the most notable Black guards in and about London.'

However, the case of Judith Defour, who was convicted in 1734, is perhaps the most sobering. She was convicted for taking her daughter out of the workhouse and strangling her in order to sell her clothes to raise money to buy gin. This shocked Victorian society to the core.

The spectre of rampant alcoholism amongst the working class terrified those in authority and gin panic set in. While legislation dealt with curbing consumption, the drinking of gin by the poorest in society was of moral concern and it wasn't long before tea was promoted as a safe and nourishing alternative.

To many Victorians, drunkenness seemed to be at the root of many evils: crime, violence, family discord, social unrest, ignorance and poverty. Temperance reformers from the late 1820s onwards attacked the problem head on by trying to get drinkers to abstain from hard liquors, and the emergence of the teetotal campaigners seeking total abstinence emerged.

Britain's temperance movement held sway in areas blighted by abject poverty, offering tea and hope to those who had fallen foul of the over-indulgence of alcohol. John Wesley was active in the eighteenth century, declaring the buying, selling and consuming of liquor evil and something to be avoided, but it wasn't until 1833 that Joseph Livesey formally introduced teetotalism to the heavily industrialised northwest

Joseph Livesey (1794-1884), social and temperance activist, writer and publisher.

of England through his Preston Temperance Society. Within a year the society had attracted 4,000 pledgers in Preston alone, all promising abstention. The teetotal movement was well under way.

Livesey was a charismatic speaker and never tired of campaigning. He remained optimistic about the possibility of a sober land, despite the number of public houses or beer houses throughout the town of Preston having increased to more than 460 by the time he delivered his temperance address for 1882.

His 1882 address delivered many poignant sentiments that lay at the heart of the prevailing Victorian views of drink depriving the poorer classes of spiritual and physical nutrition: 'What happy homes we should have if mothers would cease sending their jugs for beer; if none of our females would ever call at the dram shop or beer shop, mothers and daughters setting a good example of sobriety, cleanliness, and good household management!"

With a mixture of evangelical and philanthropic values, various Salvationists (members of the Salvation Army) preached tea and sobriety and a string of catchy temperance choruses echoed on the streets:

> Gin-sellers are plying their ruinous trade;
> Drunkards are dying and beggars are made ...

or

> Who hath woe and bitter sighing?
> Who in anguish deep do groan?
> Who in hopeless grief are crying?
> Who in dire distress do moan?

The message of the sobriety brigades could be heard up and down the country and not only did they preach the ills of liquor and ale, but the mass temperance tea parties that emerged in the 1830s and the 1840s promoted the great benefits of tea drinking. The consumption of tea, sugar and cake were championed as pleasures; ones that would lead to a religious and sober life. Mass tea parties disciplined the public through satisfying them with tea and cake and encouraging pleasurable interactions across class and gender. Temperance advocates hoped that the behaviour and values shown at the tea table would extend to the home, the factory and the marketplace. The temperance movement was a great promoter of tea being a homely, wholesome and moral beverage and contributed to the notion that drinking tea produced dutiful and motivated workers alongside rational and solvent consumers.

However, as much as tea had been taken into the hearts and homes of the British, and as much as the temperance movement championed its merits, terms such as 'tea drunkards' entered popular discourse. People also spoke of so-called 'tea mania', a peculiar late-Victorian diagnosis that was marked by an array of non-specific symptoms including headaches, vertigo, insomnia, mental confusion, nightmares, heart palpitations, nausea, hallucinations, hysteria and suicidal impulses.

As the *British Medical Journal* indicated, tea drinking seemed hazardous to health in certain contexts. A string of late-Victorian critics carved out the sharp binaries between the safe, genteel art of tea-drinking practices employed by the middle-class and the indulgent, morally dangerous tea habits that were perceived to have evolved amongst the lower classes.

A particularly prominent debate about tea erupted following the publication of a public condemnation made by the non-conformist Dean of Bangor, Henry Thomas Edwards. In 1883 Edwards interrupted a public meeting on domestic education to declare that:

> Excessive tea-drinking creates a generation of nervous, hysterical, discontented people, always complaining of the existing order of the universe, scolding their neighbours, and sighing after the impossible. Good cooking of more solid substances would, I firmly believe, enable them to take far happier and more correct views of existence. In fact I suspect that overmuch tea-drinking, by destroying the calmness of the nerves, is acting as a dangerous revolutionary force among us.

Edwards went on to elaborate on his argument against tea by insisting that 'the torrents of bad tea seem to me to be swelling into a flood of Radicalism. This bad housewifery is not only productive of possible revolution, but of lamentable immorality.'

The dean portrayed tea as a drink of anarchy explaining that, 'Once nations begin to drink tea, they lose respect for the ancient constitutions, and promote eras of reform and revolution.' Edwards also depicted the prime minister, William Gladstone, a well-known tea drinker, as 'the dread of every reactionary Conservative,' due to his reforming zeal, which he of course attributed to tea drinking

Summing up, Edwards echoed the contemporary concerns about national degeneration and tied this up with the dangers of drinking tea, branding excessive tea drinking as the cause of many complaints, including nervous excitability, physical and mental weakness and physical and mental overstimulation.

Not everyone supported this negative view of tea. Samuel Johnson was an avid tea supporter, describing himself as 'a hardened and shameless tea-drinker, who has, for twenty years, diluted his meals with only the infusion of this fascinating plant; whose kettle has scarcely time to cool; who with tea amuses the evening, with tea solaces the midnight, and, with tea, welcomes the morning.'

The quote is a well-circulated one and taken from a review Johnson wrote for *The Literary Magazine* in 1757. The work under consideration was *A Journal of Eight Days Journey from Portsmouth to Kingston upon Thames, With Miscellaneous Thoughts, Moral and Religious, in a Series of Letters*. It was a travelogue of sorts, which had been published the previous year by Jonas Hanway. Within this work was a curious piece entitled, 'An Essay on Tea', which showed that Hanway was obviously as much a hardened tea critic as Johnson was a drinker.

Hanway's claim that 'the consumption of tea is injurious to the interest of our country,' outraged Johnson and consequently he recorded a response of more than 4,000 words examining and attempting to refute Hanway's claims for the 'injurious' nature of tea. Hanway compared the 'drug called tea' to gin as being a perfidious drink promoting sloth, carelessness, and other vices: 'The late Mr. Pelham, that worthy gentleman, whose memory must we be ever grateful to this nation answered in these words: "Tea then is become another gin!" meaning as I understand it that the vast consumption, and injurous effects of tea, seemed to threaten this nation equally with gin.'

Despite Johnson's lengthy and valiant defense of tea, in 1758 an anonymous author entered the debate with a pamphlet entitled, 'The Good and Bad Effects of Tea Consider'd', which supported Hanway's arguments.The pamphlet argued that while tea drinking was acceptable for the middle and upper-classes, it should be discouraged amongst 'persons of an inferior rank and mean abilities'.

Although his argument started reasonably, pointing out that a cup of tea alone was an inadequate breakfast in terms of nutrition for those who had manual jobs to perform, it soon descended into a tirade based, like Hanway's original essay, on the belief that the social habits of the poor must be controlled and indeed curbed for the sake of the wealthier classes. He claimed that the practice of tea drinking in the afternoon amongst working-class women meant that they were 'neglecting their spinning, knitting etc spending what their husbands are labouring hard for, their children are in rags, gnawing a brown crust, while these hints, it is not my fault: but if you treat them with the refpect they deferve, I will employ all my intereft to have a ftatue erected to your memory, not of GOLD or SILVER, for I fancy we fhall want thefe metals for other purpofes, but of BRASS or MARBLE, which will laft as long.   It fhall be infcribed :

M. D C C. L V.

To

the remembrance

of the fair guardian fpirits of

B R I T A I N,

Whofe influence and example

abolifhed the ufe of

a CHINESE drug called

T E A;

the infufion of which had been for many years drank

in thefe realms and dominions,

injuring the health,

obftructing the induftry,

wafting the fortunes,

and exporting the riches,

of his MAJESTY's liege fubjects :

&c. &c.

You may now LAUGH if you pleafe ; I will laugh WITH you, provided you will alfo think ferioufly upon the fubject.   If you PRETEND to any LOVE for your country, you MUST think ferioufly.

An example of Jonas Hanway's writings on the negative effects of tea drinking.

gossips are canvassing over the affairs of the whole town, making free with the good name and reputation of their superiors.' He believed that tea encouraged these 'artful husseys' to drink spirits and to complain about their husbands, and urged innocent people to hold out against their malign influence. Unsurprisingly, this author was strongly opposed to the practice of servants receiving a tea allowance.

When tea was first introduced to Britain it was advertised as a medicine and was almost considered a panacea elixir. Thomas Garraway had claimed that tea would 'maketh the body active and lusty,' but also 'removeth the obstructions of the spleen,' and that it was 'very good against the Stone and Gravel, cleaning the Kidneys and Uriters'.

Meanwhile, the Dutch doctor Cornelius Decker had freely prescribed the consumption of tea, recommending eight to ten cups per day and claiming to drink 50-100 cups daily himself. Samuel Johnson was yet another doctor known to indulge in excessive tea drinking and was rumoured to have consumed as many as sixteen cups at one tea party. Meanwhile, in 1730, Thomas Short performed many experiments on the health effects of tea and published the results, claiming that it had curative properties against ailments such as scurvy, indigestion, chronic fear and grief. The health effects of tea were wildly debated and by the mid-eighteenth century accusations about tea's detrimental effects on health were brewing.

In a paper read to the Midland Scientific Association in 1863, physician Dr Edwin Brown claimed that British physical stamina, which had formerly been strong compared to that of other countries, had dramatically declined. To illustrate his argument, Brown reminded his audience that the present-day Chinese were merely 'degenerate representations of their ancestors, who, prior to their being a tea-drinking nation, carried fire and sword over large portions of Europe and Asia.' Brown did not mention the fact that British policy had produced millions of opium addicts, reducing China to a corrupt and demoralised society, while ruining the stability of the Chinese economy. Brown's focus was on the undermining nature of tea. For him, the weakening effects of tea had been a prime contributor to Chinese decadence and racial decline. The key target of Brown's anxieties was specifically caffeine, a substance presented as sapping strength and being able to result in paralysis.

Tea wasn't even considered safe within the confines of the temperance society. The Anglican minister, John Wesley, condemned it for its

A line drawing of an opium den, as featured in the *Illustrated London News*.

stimulant properties, stating that it was harmful to the body and soul and could cause numerous nervous disorders. Wesley even offered advice on how to deal with the awkward social situation of declining the offer of taking tea.

Controversially, in 1872 the pioneer of occupational medicine, John Thomas Arlidge, argued that the reforming zeal of the temperance movement needed to be directed to the repression of 'tea-tippling' amongst the poor. Arlidge considered tea to be as harmful and addictive as alcohol. He argued that if opium and alcohol were to be classified as narcotic poisons, then so should tea as it ruined digestion, weakened the heart, and destroyed the nerves. According to Arlidge, it was 'a form of animal indulgence which is as distinctly sensual, extravagant and pernicious as any beer-swilling or gin drinking in the world.'

Debates about health, nutrition and the financial burden of tea on the poor were pondered upon at length. Dr Thomas Short harboured grave concerns that poor families were putting tea above nutrition, leading to disastrous ailments. He argued that people would spend money on tea rather than food and were consequently jeopardizing their health.

Mid-Victorian society seemed to struggle to reconcile its complex, often contradictory, views on tea. As the middle-class obsession with tea grew and tea parties boomed, it was hard to ignore the fact that increased access to the product throughout the social strata had led to it becoming a necessity, as opposed to a luxury, amongst less affluent sections of society, giving rise to concern over the health and strength of the working classes if they were favouring tea over bread.

Meanwhile, physicians continued to diagnose women with an array of nervous symptoms with the overdosing of tea. In particular, chronic dyspepsia was frequently upheld as the emblematic symptom of poor nutritional choices and excessive tea-drinking habits. A married woman was expected to nurture, feed and preserve the health of her family. Concerns mounted over the inability of many women to fulfil their household duties due to tea intoxication.

The complaints of vague symptoms from women of all ranks of society were attributed to tea drinking. Everything from headaches, nausea and loss of appetite to physical distress after eating and chronic dizziness were all attributed to excessive tea drinking. The practice of keeping a teapot stewing and taking regular drinks from it was frowned upon.

This negative dialogue about the damaging effects of tea as debated by the medical profession did not go unnoticed by the authorities and coroners were known to reach verdicts of 'death by tea poisoning'. This was the case in Poplar in 1869, when evidence suggested that a thirty-eight-year old male furniture dealer who had drank as much as eight cups of tea before leaving home in the morning had unwittingly destroyed his nervous system, resulting in his death.

Victorian England was no stranger to the belief that death could be caused by the consumption of tea and this was typically used as a cover by those with their minds on insurance money. Mary Ann Cotton, hanged in 1873 for the murder of her stepson, Charles Edward Cotton, is thought to have murdered fifteen members of her family, including three of her four husbands and eleven of her thirteen children. She used arsenic to poison her victims, administered in a comforting cup of tea made in a small teapot which she reserved for the deadly purpose.

The notion of death by tea poisoning also saved others from the gallows. During the hearing of a woman charged with the wilful murder of her two children at the Waltham Abbey Petty Sessions in 1891, evidence revealed that the accused mother had become fixated on the idea that her children were desperately ill and about to perish. Doctor Fulcer, who examined the accused, determined that the unfortunate mother had suffered from a weak heart, headaches, palpitation and sleeplessness, the consequences of a persistent tea-drinking habit. The doctor diagnosed that excessive tea drinking had weakened the woman's mental condition. 'There is little doubt,' reported *The Lancet* on the incident, 'that in a woman of a neurotic temperament, especially if her food were deficient in quantity and of poor quality, the use of this beverage in excess would be one of the factors in producing and perpetuating a condition of mental instability.'

The debate about the health and social implications of drinking tea continued to rage, but consumption remained high. While some continued to have a violent prejudice against tea, in the 1820s the Scottish physician Sir Gilbert Blane, known for his reforms in naval hygiene and medicine, remarked, 'Tea is an article universally grateful to the British population and has to a certain extent supplanted intoxicating liquors in all ranks, to the great advantage of society [...] tea has probably contributed to the longevity of the inhabitants of this country.' The physician advised the extension of the use of tea in the navy.

Though there was some basis for the concerns about decreased levels of nutrition in the poor as a result of tea drinking, in as much as tea was

The Victorian serial killer, Mary Ann Cotton, who claimed the lives of her victims with her arsenic-filled teapot.

less nutritious than beer, the fact remained that drinking tea also carried health benefits. It had replaced more damaging beverages such as rough gin. It had become part of the daily diet of the average person by the latter part of the eighteenth century. Labourers were spending ten per cent of their food budgets on tea and sugar, twelve per cent on meat and cheese and only two and half per cent on beer. Tea was a warming drink that helped to supplement the meagre diets of the lower classes. The living conditions of the poor were insalubrious and countless reports commend the heartening effects of tea on those who faced daily misfortune.

Though deteriorating health and wellbeing of the poor continued to be blamed on the consumption of tea by some eighteenth century critics, its benefits during times of great hardship were becoming increasingly well documented in the nineteenth century. The statistician John Rickman wrote in 1827 on the subject of mortality rates: 'It is not for Mr Rickman to assign causes of the decrease of mortality; if he might venture further than in the Preliminary Observations to the Census of 1811 and 1821 he would ascribe it to the general use of tea and sugar.'

The positive impact of drinking tea during times of war were also being reported. Florence Nightingale noted the beneficial effects of tea on the wounded and dispirited soldiers who flooded into the field hospitals. In her book *Directions for Cooking by Troops, in Camp and Hospital* she stated that, 'there is nothing yet discovered which is a substitute to the English patient for his cup of tea.'

With time, the fears of tea and its health warnings faded as new food legislation laws clamped down on tea adulteration. Tea has continued to establish itself as a British necessity, giving comfort, happiness and warmth. It has provided the rich with social grace and thrown the poor a lifeline with which to struggle through another hard day. Tea has started wars and comforted people in times of war.

Raging debates over the benefits of tea still go on today. Opinions on which type of tea is healthier, how many cups we should be drinking each day, or whether the anti-oxidants in tea are anti-ageing, are all very much the subject of national debate. As is the debate over how you actually make it: loose leaf or bag; bag in or bag out; tea pot or mug; milk first or milk after. The politics of tea making are constantly on the boil and the whistle hasn't blown yet on the debate over how tea drinking actually affects us.

Chapter 7

The British Tradition of Tea

Tea and the British have become almost synonymous, but though much was made of trying this new and exotic drink that was being advertised as a powerful curative remedy, it was quite some time before anyone mentioned actually enjoying it.

During the first 150 years of tea drinking in Britain the tea leaf was treated as a rare and expensive luxury. Tea drinking was still considered an avant-garde activity at this time, and anyone from the upper classes who wished to be fashionable would drink it simply to keep abreast of continental vogue, regardless of its taste.

It is likely that the quality of the tea that arrived in the late seventeenth century was not conducive to an agreeable flavor as it was often stale and usually adulterated with inferior leaves. Furthermore, tea did not initially receive the proper preparatory treatment that might have improved its taste. In the seventeenth century methods of preparing tea had not developed into the refined processes of later years. The British did not yet know how hot to boil water to make tea, or how long to steep the leaves for. Tea leaves were boiled up in bulk and the resulting brew was placed into a wooden barrel to be drawn off in a similar way to ale. Thankfully, the quality of tea and its preparation improved and by 1750 it was on its way to becoming the British favourite that it is today.

In 1813 the East India Company lost its trade monopoly on India, but retained its monopoly on trade with China, which meant the company was heavily dependent on the profits from the Chinese tea trade. The Company's charter granting the Chinese trade monopoly was due for renewal in 1834, and in the decades prior to that there was a growing call for the abolition of the monopoly and the instigation of free trade with China. The cries for free trade were getting louder as many argued that the monopoly was keeping tea prices artificially high in order to bolster the Company's profits. There were also allegations of the Company using underhand tactics such as restricting the supply of tea.

One anonymous pro-freetrade writer in 1824 stated that 'the lordly grocers of Leadenhall Street [where the East India Company was based] have most scandalously abused the monopoly of which they are now in possession.' Comparing the prices of tea sold at auction in London with the prices at auction in Hamburg and New York, the writer launched a scathing attack stating that 'the monopoly of the tea trade enjoyed by the East India Company costs the people of this country, on average, not less than TWO MILLION TWO HUNDRED THOUSAND pounds sterling a year!'

It was inevitable that the trade monopoly would fall under the weight of public opinion and in light of the Company's jaded track record its future was precarious. In 1834 Parliament's new charter for the Company abolished its trading functions altogether. Instead, the Company became an agent of the British government, administering British India on behalf of the Crown. India was still to be ruled from the boardroom

PUNCH, OR THE LONDON CHARIVARI.—MAY 7, 1919.

IMPERIAL PREFERENCE.

The great tea divide: illustrating the preference Britain had for British Colonial tea.

of the East India Company, but its rulers would no longer also be tea dealers. China was still the major source of tea, but as the Company had now been relieved of any trading rights with China, its thoughts turned to the possibility of growing tea in India. Until this point the Company had been given no incentive to cultivate the leaf outside of China. It was to become one of the most significant turning points in the history of British tea.

A committee was established to investigate where in India might be most suitable for the cultivation of tea plants. One obvious area was Assam, where indigenous tea plants had already been found growing. Seeds from China were germinated in Calcutta and then sent on to Assam and other areas to conduct trials. C.A. Bruce, an agent of the East India Company in Assam, was appointed Superintendent of Tea Forests and set about cultivating plantations of both Chinese and indigenous tea. The British had to learn growing techniques, something that is evident from the variations between the ancient Chinese methods of cultivation and processing and the ones that came to be employed in Assam. The British integrated machines into the stages of cultivating, processing, and packaging tea, and it was these new cultivating and processing methods that made the new tea industry in Assam distinctly British.

In 1838 twelve chests of Assam tea were sent to the East India Company in London. Some was used for promotion and as samples to build trade interest, and the rest went to the regular London Tea Auction. This was the first auction of Assam tea in London, and the novelty of the product ensured that it reached a good price. This auction was held on 10 January 1839 and saw the sale of eight chests. The second sale of Assam tea was advertised in the London auction catalogue advertised as 'Asam Tea. 85 Packages. For Sale, by Order of the Honourable East India Company [...] March Sales, 1840.' The offering of this exotic variety of tea would have caused a stir with fashionable tea merchants who saw an opportunity to offer their customers something rare. H.A. Antrobus, in *History of the Assam Company* (1957), writes that this second batch of Assam tea was still the product of 'meere patches of indigenous tea trees found in the jungle and cut down to about 3ft. from the ground'.

These first two sales were important in the history of what would become a very British tea trade, as it marked the beginning of the British-designed Indian tea industry, which was set to go from strength to strength. In 1842 William James Bland noted in issue 83 of his regular

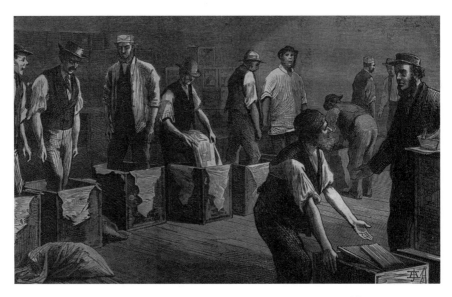

An artistic depiction of a tea warehouse, in which chests were refilled.

report on the quality of the teas being auctioned, that 'The Assam Teas [are] a decided improvement on all previous shipments in this one particularly – viz, that the crude flavour which added an objectionable strength has been dissipated by an altered preparation'. By 1862 it is estimated that India was producing over one and a half million pounds of tea annually.

The London Tea Auction started in 1679 with the first auctions held by the East India Company. They were held at the headquarters of the Company on Leadenhall Street, which came to be known as East India House. Held quarterly, these auctions were lively affairs, where the tea was sold by 'candle'. This meant that, rather than allowing bidding to go on for an unlimited length of time, a candle was lit at the beginning of the sale of each lot, and when an inch of the candle had burnt away, the hammer fell and the sale for that lot was concluded.

In the late seventeenth century, the auctions sold other imported goods, primarily fabrics and piece goods that the Company had brought back from the East. The auction of fine and exotic goods caused a lively atmosphere, with bidding and jostling. By the early eighteenth century, however, tea was so popular that the London Tea Auction came into its own and the focus of this quarterly auction became reserved solely for tea.

Things had to change. The East India Company had controlled the auctions due to their monopoly on the tea trade, but in 1834, when the East India Company ceased to be a commercial enterprise and tea became a 'free-trade' commodity, the auction needed to be rehomed. The East India Company liquidated their stocks at the last sale held in their offices in July 1835 and the tea auctions now came under the tea traders' own control. They left the splendour of East India House, with the echoes of past auctions still audible, and took up temporary residence in a room in Change Alley that was usually used as a dance studio.

Large quantities of free-trade teas began to arrive from India and the auctions set up home in the newly built London Commercial Salerooms on Mincing Lane, where it would reside until 1935. Within a few years various tea merchants established offices at Mincing Lane, earning it the nickname the 'Street of Tea'.

By the middle of the nineteenth century tea was such a popular beverage that quarterly auctions were no longer sufficient; they began to take place monthly, and then weekly. The world of tea was moving fast and soon the tradition of selling 'by the candle' was replaced by more modern methods. London attracted widespread buying interest, where teas from a great variety of producing countries were regularly offered in competition with one another.

In 1935 the London Tea Auctions were to move home again, this time to swanky Plantation House, built in the 1930s and the city's second largest building at the time. Covering a major site on Fenchurch Street, the building was designed by Albert W. Moore to house the tea trade's commodity traders all under one roof: the tea plantation companies, the brokers, the shippers and even allied industries like sugar, timber and rubber were all housed at these impressive premises. At one stage it was the recognised centre of the world's tea trade, but all good things come to an end and Plantation House was demolished in 1991. The London Tea Auctions had already vacated the premises over a decade previously and were operating from Sir John Lyon House. The auction rooms now had a panoramic view overlooking the Thames, where the ghosts of clippers loaded with chests of tea returning from British-owned plantations in the Orient could be imagined.

Because of its strategic location, London provided a centre for the re-export of tea to over fifty destinations. Tea was sent from India, China, Ceylon and Africa for sale at the auction, and as the auction continued to flourish it introduced the practice of devoting particular days of the

The J. Lyons Tea Rooms, situated in Queens Square, Wolverhampton, Staffordshire. These were popular tea rooms where the teashop waitresses in their smart black and white uniforms were known as Nippies from 1924 onwards. All Nippies were deft at serving tea, handling crockery and giving out smiles. These tea establishments were popular not just with ladies, but with gentleman suitors looking for a wife. *The Picture Post* in 1939 reported that there were a total of between 800 and 900 Nippy marriages every year. Lyons claimed that the marriage rate among Nippies was higher than any other class of working girl because the job was excellent training for a housewife.

week to the sale of teas from each individual country. London was at the centre of the world's tea sales and by the 1950s a third of the world's tea was bought through the auction. Once purchased, the tea was sent from London warehouses, directly to retailers where it was sold loose, or to companies that specialised in blending and packaging. These companies then sold the tea ready packed under various brand names, offering a wide range of choice to tea drinkers.

No one could have predicted the power and lasting control that the market would have when the East India Company held the first auction in 1679, where it sold three casks of 'dust of thea' from China for £1 and 11s. The auctions had grown steadily and consistently and a catalogue for one of the East India Company's quarterly sales in 1798 contained 635 pages of offerings, with each chest of tea inspected and sampled by company experts. The London Tea Auctions looked to be invincible.

Tea blending at the Cutler Street warehouse.

Indeed, the auction system was acclaimed as the universal model for the marketing of tea. The inauguration of the auctions in London helped to establish a global network of tea auctions in most producer countries, thereby creating a world market for tea; an arrangement that worked perfectly as long as the world's tea production was under British control. Even after Britain's tea-producing colonies won their independence, the weekly London auctions remained a focal point for the global industry and continued to do a steady trade, though the signs of decline were already in evidence. Even into the 1970s, fifteen percent of the world's tea was traded in London, but this was a far cry from the days when auctions were so busy that there was barely standing room.

Prior to the Second World War, more than sixty percent of teas produced by British interests the world over were marketed in London, but with India, Ceylon and Kenya becoming independent in 1947, 1948 and 1963 respectively, London was soon to lose its position as the dominant player in the tea trade. After the war, the London Tea Auctions did not reopen until 1951, whereas sales were resumed in Calcutta in 1946 and in Colombo in 1947. Most producer countries, after having taken their cue from Britain, were quick to develop their own methods of marketing and selling tea, all of which was done at the expense of London. The postwar period witnessed a sharp drop in the quantities consigned for London auctions as the sales in producer countries increased.

London was unable to compete as the marketing of tea in the countries of origin had a significant advantage for the producers: savings on shipping costs and the ability to convert their crops into cash quickly. London was fast losing its importance as a source of supply to the British consumer and the free-trade that had once boosted London's share now brought about its demise.

Other factors, such as a reduction in British consumption, consolidation in the tea trade, the increasing power of large international tea packers and marketers such as Unilever and Tetley, alongside changes in communications all contributed to the demise of the tea auctions. As British buyers began to trade with producers via telephone and fax, abandoning floor-based trading in favour of electronic dealing, the number of London brokers who served as middlemen also declined: in 1959 there were twelve tea brokers in London, but by the late 1990s there were only two.

On the 29 June 1998 the very last London Tea Auction took place, marking the diminished role of Britain in a trade it had nurtured. The last sale was held in a rented room at London's Chamber of Commerce, with only 407 tons of tea being auctioned, whereas in previous decades a typical day's auction sale would have seen 1,000 tons fall under the gavel. A chapter of British tea history concluded and the last sale took just forty-five minutes to complete; a far cry from the sales of the 1900s, where the volume of tea was so high that each week Indian teas were auctioned off on Mondays and Wednesdays, Ceylon teas on Tuesdays, and China, Java and other teas on Thursdays. The last lot of tea to be sold at the London auction was a chest of Ceylon Flowery Pekoe from the Hellbodde Tea Estate, which achieved the price of £555 per kilo, making it the most expensive tea to be sold at auction (perhaps because this tea was a piece of history and marked the end of a very important chapter in British tea).

As the gavel fell for the last time at the London Tea Auction the ghosts of London's tea warehouses were also laid to rest. There had been a time when teas were auctioned at Mincing Lane before leaving the warehouses that surrounded the Port of London and being transported to the blenders. London had been a central player in the import, sale, storage and distribution of tea.

TEA

FOR SALE,

AT THE

London Commercial Sale Rooms,

MINCING LANE,

On TUESDAY, 2nd April, 1839.

42	Half-Chests	Orange Pekoe
54	Chests	} Twankay.
18	Half-Chests	}
123	Chests	} Hyson
30	Half-Chests	}
23	Half-Chests	Young Hyson
6	Chests	Gunpowder
296	**Packages**	

W. E. FRANKS,

BROKER,

25, FENCHURCH STREET.

PRINTED BY E. TEAPE AND SON, TOWER HILL.

A tea auction catalogue from 2 April 1839.

In 1768 the East India Company purchased land on New Street for the purpose of warehousing. Its first building was named the Bengal Warehouse and housed textiles from Bengal. Further parcels of land were purchased and more warehouses were constructed up until 1820, by which stage the Company owned most of the area that Devonshire Square Estate occupies today. The Company used the warehouses mainly

Expensive imported ostrich feathers being processed at the Cutler Street warehouse.

for the storage of tea and at its height the complex saw the employment of 400 clerks and some 4,000 warehousemen.

When the East India Company's trade monopoly ceased in the 1830s, the warehouses were sold to the St Katharine Dock Company. Then in 1909 they changed hands again when they were acquired by the Port of London Authority, which at this time was the most dominant warehouse keeper in the world.

The most valuable goods were stored in the Cutler Street warehouses, where the forbidding fortress-like walls and the fire-proof construction afforded excellent protection. The Cutler Street warehouses covered four acres and had a floor area of 630,000sq ft. They housed all sorts of exotic wares including ostrich feathers, ivory, spices, cochineal, oriental carpets, cigars, tortoiseshell, silks, mother of pearl, perfumes, tea and other prized commodities, including ivory for the London Market. In 1896 it was recorded in *The Queen's London* that 'Twenty thousand tons of goods can be housed on the premises, representing a value of between three and four million sterling.'

Cutler Street became the premier tea warehouse for the Port of London Authority at one stage. Tea was stored, blended, packed and shipped from its warehouses. It was not unusual to see men with wooden shovels turning over thousands of pounds of tea and mixing it to make popular blends. By the 1950s most of the tea business operations had been moved to the London Dock, and the vacated space was occupied by casks of wine, port and sherry. The rapid changes in transportation methods signalled a change from warehouse space to shipping containers in the 1970s. This, coupled with the decline in tea auctions, meant that the warehouses were no longer needed and the complexes gradually declined. The Cutler Street warehouses were the last to remain in use by the Port of London Authority, but by 1978 everything had closed.

It is ironic that the plantations which Britain had strived to develop ultimately spelled the death of London as the centre of world tea trade. After the dissolution of the trade monopoly in 1834, new companies that developed in its wake were able to thrive. Competition after 1834 allowed the growth of the tea trade amongst independent British merchants, and they contributed to the then rapidly increasing British tea trade. The fall of London's Tea Auction marked the end of a 300-year-old tradition and also the end of London's history as an influencer in the world of tea.

The formation of the Assam Company had marked an exciting time in the history of British tea and while the Assam Company faced many

The Cutler Street warehouse today.

challenges in setting up the new tea plantation, by 1855 tea cultivation in the northeastern Indian state amounted to over half a million pounds. But as was the pattern throughout the history of British involvement with tea, trouble was brewing.

Though the East India Company had lost its trading rights, it had not lost its commercial appetite. The cost of the Company's Indian administration was met through heavy taxation and charges on the Indian people and this led to localised rebellions. The Company resorted to increasingly heavy-handed tactics to control the local population, but in May 1857 three regiments of Indian soldiers serving in the Company's army at Meerut near Delhi rebelled. The revolt spread and led to a brutal conflict as the British forces tried to extinguish it. Despite the Company's efforts, the rebellion raged for over a year, during which time both sides committed atrocities. After peace was achieved the trust between the Indians and the East India Company administration was destroyed and a disillusioned British government decided to dissolve the East India Company and directly assume all its powers and possessions in India. The first viceroy, Lord Canning, was appointed to govern British India.

The glory years of the East India Company were over but the rise of Indian tea production had not yet peaked. With the exception of Darjeeling, which was producing high-quality but low-yielding tea crops, there was little cultivation outside Assam. The new British administration in India saw the potential for more widespread cultivation and offered generous land leases to potential tea planters. By 1888 the annual Indian tea production had reached £86 million and for the first time British tea imports from India exceeded those from China. A very British tea romance had begun. Great hopes for the British Empire were placed on Assam, but the course of true love never runs smoothly and it took many years for Assam's tea trade to become efficient and effective.

British merchants, investors and the tea-loving British public were all benefactors of the success of the Assam tea trade, but it destroyed the Chinese export market to Britain. By 1900 there were no recorded shipments of tea coming into London from China. The Indian tea industry was now outperforming China's, and American and Dutch invaders would soon enter Chinese tea regions to strip them of their seeds and their ancient practices. The Chinese workers who had relied on tea for their livelihoods had no lifeline and China's annual tea production fell dramatically to 41,000 tons by 1949.

Tea in Britain had received an image transformation. For years it had been a foreign product with which British society was familiar. Indeed, it was the British style of drinking tea that conjured up images for many of the British way of life. And when India's tea trade was started its cultivation became wholly British. The new tea industry that began in the 1830s was British-controlled and relied on no Chinese input, equipment, or knowledge. Tea cultivation was a closely guarded secret in China, so the British devised their own methods based on horticultural observation and introduced manufacturing to the processing of tea. As the new British style of tea was taking off and tea drinking itself was now considered a very British institution, sales began to increase and new avenues were explored.

The idea of taking tea was well and truly integrated into existing daily routines. People's lives began to change to accommodate their much-needed cuppa. Tea had moved away from the confines of the male coffee-house and was increasingly consumed at home. Specialist blenders became more popular and more tea merchants opened throughout the land with their distinctly British interiors and shop fittings similar to those in chemists and grocers of the time, thus divorcing tea from its oriental roots and claiming it as a purely British commodity.

Budget & Budget, a Bristol-based company, opened their tea and coffee shop in Queen Street, Wolverhampton in the 1830s. Like so many tea merchants, it was to prove popular. The company grew and managed to build up a chain of 100 shops before being sold and changing hands until, at the end of the 1800s, it was bought by a Mr Snape who took over and gave the business his own name. This new name would be retained until it eventually shut its doors for good in 2002.

When Mr Snape died just after the Second World War, he passed the business on to his employee, Albert Edward Parkes, who kept the name W.T.M. Snape. In turn Albert passed the business on to his son, Tom, who in turn left the business to his son, Philip, who was the final owner of the business.

During the eighteenth and nineteenth century, tea merchants like Snape would not have been exceptional. Their establishments were commonplace trading posts in which knowledgeable merchants would hand blend teas from their fine selection. With its long mahogany counter, brass scales and hand-painted tea canisters, the tea and coffee shop of W.T.M. Snape of Wolverhampton presented a sepia-tinged image of a

A very British advert, promoting the imperialistic qualities of tea.

forgotten era. With its ornate gas light fittings and display of tea bins that had arrived in Britain on the *Cutty Sark*, the shop paid homage to a lost age of tea splendor. Indeed, the shop's only concession to the modern age was the introduction of electricity in the 1970s. As the interior of the shop remained entirely original, so did the service, with the owner doing his own tasting and blending and serving customers individually in the time-honoured practice.

Snape's witnessed the evolution of tea from its days as an expensive commodity kept in elaborate caddies in drawing rooms, to its growing ubiquity in the kitchen cupboards of the working classes. They saw the move from loose-leaf to brand-named tea and of course the introduction of teabags. They tracked the changes in tea-drinking fashions, survived tea rationing during two world wars (when they had to diversify by selling jam and sugar alongside tea) and witnessed the stranglehold of tea over British culture and society loosen. The caricature of Britain as a tea-obsessed nation is far from a fictional one.

Throughout history we have laughed, cried, celebrated, sighed with relief, debated and gossiped over the stuff, but since 1974 the purchase of household tea began to decline: in 1974 an average person would drink twenty-three cups a week, whereas nearly four decades later weekly consumption was down to just eight cups. No doubt Snape's would have been dismayed at the shift from the lovingly brewed tea in a china cup to a quick-fix tea made in a mug. Like the tea auctions and warehouses of London, the traditional tea merchant struggled to maintain the appeal of their illustrious past. And so, after enjoying over 170 years of trade, W.T.M Snape ceased to be a source of nostalgia and a tea stop for discerning palates. The old-fashioned ways of hand blending, along with a wealth of knowledge and a standard of service were lost to history as another victim of change was claimed.

Advertising and the introduction of name-brand tea in Britain reinforced the established notion of this beloved beverage as Britain's national drink. The changes that started in the 1830s, both in terms of the new processing techniques and marketing, completed the long process of making tea completely British. The humble leaf had been on a very long journey in order to become British, one that saw it subjected to changes and adaptations on social, commercial, and industrial levels.

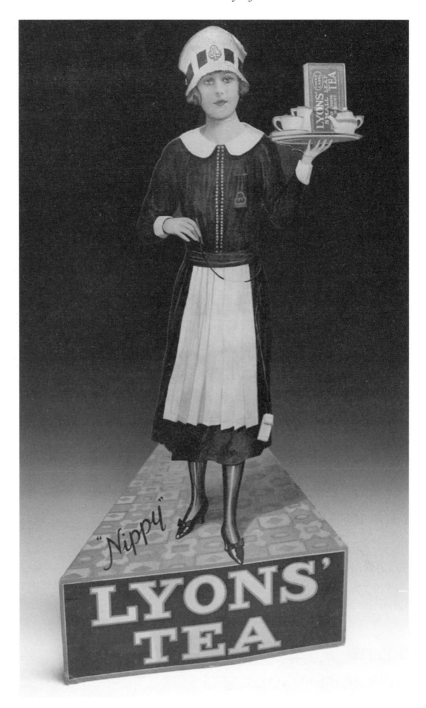

A Lyon's advertisement, using the popular and iconic image of a Nippy.

An advertisement for tea, emphasizing its quality as a British commodity.

The critics would now be silenced. Tea had fulfilled the requirements to become a national beverage and its growing popularity enabled independent traders to flourish and create a new industry in the wake of the demise of the East India Company's monopoly in 1834, when tea

An illustration portraying an idyllic Indian tea seed garden.

was still a Chinese product and still considered foreign and too exotic for many tastes.

The road to becoming wholly and recognisably British began with the completion of the newly founded British tea industry in India; the final step in Britain's claim to tea as part of our national identity. Tea from India was marketed as superior compared to that of China in terms of purity and quality. *The Queens Empire: A Pictorial and Descriptive Record of 1897* features a piece on Assam tea that states: 'the excellent quality of the Indian tea is too familiar to need description. British activity and intelligence have multiplied the tea garden and improved the quality of the leaf'.

Indian tea growing was depicted as idyllic and the focus in reports was placed on how the British had applied ingenuity to improve tea output and quality. There was no mention that tea producing is very labour intensive. When tea plantation workers are portrayed they are always serenely picking tea tips and smiling, without a hint of the arduous life that they have to endure. When the East India Company first established the tea gardens in Assam they recognised how labour intensive the process was. The obvious solution would have been to use slaves, but in 1833 slavery was banned in the British Empire, so an alternative had to be found.

Instead of slaves, tea estates used indentured labourers; free men and women who signed contracts binding them to work for a certain period. The pretty pictures that have appeared on tea packets of happy women in saris, set against a backdrop of rolling green hills, was a world away from the reality of these workers' daily lives. Low wages, long working hours, poor living conditions, lack of adequate sanitation, disease and malnutrition were all part of the tea picker's life and they were treated no better than slaves.

It was very much in the interests of tea growers and traders to portray Indian workers in a clean working environment in order to reinforce their message of good quality, pure tea. A tea merchant's card from 1912, describes, 'Indian tea is dried by clean currents of hot air. The essential elements are thus fixed on the surface of the leaf and the flavour and aroma are complete.' The merchant, H. Lazell of Colchester, reminds customers to take note of his tea display and it is certain that for many customers the only vision they would have of India would be that imagined on the advertisements for their tea.

Fears of adulteration had been circulating for as long as tea had been popular and whilst this fear was partly quelled by the drinking of black

Tea pluckers, photographed in 1900.

tea, the promise that Indian tea was purer, better quality and came with a British assurance, was popular with consumers. Manufacturers were keen to exploit this new opportunity to influence consumers and win their customer loyalty.

The industrial revolution and the emergence of the middle class in Victorian Britain led to an unprecedented rise of supply and demand for consumer goods. To promote their products, small entrepreneurs started to adopt new marketing strategies, including branding and advertising. As a result, advertisements became increasingly common in newspapers, magazines and books.

The importance of the middle class cannot be understated in the growth of tea. Without a ready market there would have been no outlet for increasing tea sales. It was the newly enriched middle class whose incomes had risen as mass production had lowered the cost of necessities. This meant they had more money to spend on luxuries than ever before. The message from advertisers of teas was clear: the best and purest tea came from India.

An increasing market with an inflated budget was matched by the growing number of manufacturers, so companies had to compete for their share by making sure their advertisements were going to be noticed. At the same time new machines were being invented to allow a finer quality of printing, which allowed a boost in terms of the quality and creativity of the advertisements seen in the Victorian era. These factors led to an explosion of advertising and some powerful and long lasting branding.

The industrial revolution and Britain's imperial ambitions resulted in a geographical expansion of markets. An

A Mazawattee tea advertisement, 1890.

influx of goods from around the world and the opportunity to promote British products farther afield meant new impetus and possibilities for advertisers. Advertising was gaining momentum and soon every grocer's store was filled with show cards promoting everything from tea to treacle, while publications advertised food and drinks from far-off places alongside exciting new inventions such as the ballpoint pen and medical aids.

The British Empire was at its peak and the world of advertising was expanding as newly colonised countries provided a constant source of inspiration as well as new goods. In the same way that the British justified their imperial expansion through the theory of the 'white man's burden', bringing civilisation and an advanced culture to their new colonies, so too did advertisers promote their products with the message of moral goodness at its heart. This was a time of massive technological innovation: new machines and industries were transforming the world by making wonderful products. The language used in advertising campaigns was full of optimism, based on the claim that science and industry would solve all the problems of poverty, hunger, and disease.

As manufacturers strove to find ways to differentiate themselves from one another and influence consumers to buy their products rather than their competitors', they tried to create effective advertising campaigns involving the use of targeted slogans, images, and phrases. In the late nineteenth century the marketing of 'pure' became ever more apparent. Amidst fears that unpackaged goods could not be trusted, that bread was not wholesome and milk might be watered down, concerned mothers and housewives were drawn to the 'pure' and 'wholesome' claims used in the adverts. Advertisers cleverly equated the purity of a food product with a physical, mental or spiritual purity. In doing so, they invested their food with a moral authority and legitimacy that led Victorian consumers to buy into the lifestyle and cultural value that the products promised. Typically the idealised 'perfect' family image was used to appeal to those wanting to please their husbands, protect their children and create a happy home environment.

While trusted tea merchants were still popular, the everyday householder could now purchase hygienically wrapped, sealed bags of tea from grocers. Consumers could feel safe in the knowledge that

An advertisement label from 1892. Wholesome images of family life were popular, communicating an idea of purity and goodness that consumers were eager to buy into.

they were getting what they paid for and that its contents were pure. They were suddenly able to choose the brand of tea they wanted, based on price, taste and value, as well as the various promises and assurances made in the adverts.

This was a time when 'shopping' referred to obtaining the necessities of life and the reign of the independent grocer was alive and well. The lives of those from either side of the counter were intertwined as the shopkeeper relied on the customers' loyal patronage and the customers relied on the local grocer for supplies. These shops with their pigeon hole shelving, array of drawers, assortment of goods, dim lighting and personal service represent a way of life and shopping that is now a distant memory. However, in an age when trading standards had yet to be introduced (until the 1870s there were no laws guaranteeing the quality of goods) some grocers were known to employ sharp practices. While butchers disguised rancid meat by painting it with chemicals, bakers bulked up expensive flour with chalk and alum and grocers added gravel to coffee and an array of substances to tea. All of these practices were soon to become less widespread as advertisers promoted wholesomeness and consumers began to demand products by brand. Improved wage-earning opportunities for women and children boosted family spending. Suddenly people could afford more staples such as tea, butter, bread, milk, beer, cheese, meat, vegetables, fruit and fish. The demand for goods was fuelling growth and there was an increase in the number of urban and village shops.

Throughout the 1800s and into the first half of the twentieth century, the independent retailer was a cornerstone of British life. It was commonplace for people to buy groceries on a daily basis and for visits to the local grocer to be a routine part of life. But while the traditional grocer's goods were weighed out by hand, cut up, sliced and bundled, grocers increasingly became heavily weighted towards branded goods and their shelves and displays became more vivid as their shops became a playground for manufactures to compete for custom.

The country had switched allegiance from green tea to black and the nineteenth century saw Indian tea imports into Britain overtake the imports from China, but many other changes were happening in the world of tea. There were major changes in where tea was drunk and by whom, there was a rise in branded teas gaining loyalties over grocers' own blends, and the twentieth century introduced something that would radically change our tea-drinking habits forever: the tea bag.

The invention of the tea bag is said to have been a happy accident, when, around 1908, Thomas Sullivan, a New York tea merchant, started to send samples of tea to his customers in small silken bags. Some customers mistakenly assumed that these were supposed to be used in the same way as tea infusers, and placed the entire bag into their teapots rather than emptying out the contents. And so the concept of the tea bag was born.

Responding to the comments from his customers that the mesh on the silk was too fine, Sullivan developed sachets made of gauze, and after some experimentation they were commercially ready. However, material shortages during the Second World War held up production plans and it wasn't until after the war that the tea bag really became popular. In an era of inventions for household convenience and labour-saving devices, the tea bag was the ideal partner for the 1950's American ideal of effortless housekeeping.

A vintage advertisement for Tetley tea bags.

There is, however another contender for the title of tea bag inventor. Seven years earlier Roberta C. Lawson and Mary Molaren of Milwaukee filed for a patent for a 'tea leaf holder' that also resembles what we call a tea bag today. 'By this means,' they wrote, 'only so much of tea-leaves is used as is required for the single cup of tea,' thus making less waste. As they detailed in their application, the bag needed to hold the tea leaves together so that they didn't float into the drinker's mouth, but not hold them so tightly that the water was prevented from circulating through them to be infused. Their design used a stitched mesh fabric.

Regardless of the identity of the real inventor, the tea bag solved two problems: how to make single-serving tea brewing more convenient and how to reduce tea preparation time. While the American population enthusiastically embraced the tea bag, the British, with their regimented tea-making rituals, were naturally wary of such a radical method. In 1930 William Hermanson patented the heat-sealed tea bag, but it was only after the Second World War, when Joseph Tetley and Company began to mass-produce tea bags in 1953, that the British adopted the concept. The following year the *Stock Exchange Gazette* wrote that Joseph Tetley was 'particularly well known for the introduction of tea packed in small bags for immediate use in a pot.'

In 1931 William McKercher, superintendent of the Amgoorie Tea Estate in Assam, revolutionised the manufacture of black tea by inventing the crush, tear and curl processing method. This would change the character of tea brewing. Rather than rolling and twisting the leaves in the traditional manner, a machine cut them into small pieces. The resulting pebbly granules not only produced a quicker and stronger brew, but were also a lot more convenient for filling tea bags. The crush, tear and curl method gained popularity in the mid-twentieth century alongside the tea bag. Today, approximately ninety-five per cent of the world's black tea is produced using McKercher's method.

As stated above, the tea bag was not an immediate success with the British, who believed that it contained the sweepings from factory floors, that it was made from tea dust and that it generally contained tea of an inferior quality. The tea bag was seen as another American abomination, like chewing gum. Even as late as the early 1960s they accounted for just three percent of the market. Convinced that the tea bag was the future because of the way it allowed the tea maximum exposure to the water, resulting in a good, strong brew, Tetley persevered with perfecting the tea bag and overcame the issue of finding a tissue that did not taint the tea. In 1964, the finely perforated bag was developed and improved the tea bag's image. While it remained the object of scorn to hardened tea connoisseurs, it began to fly off the shelves and made its way into the British pot.

Persuading the British to change their tea-drinking habits from loose tea was a challenge. Tetley promoted tea bags as being the new quick and easy way to make a delicious cup of tea for only one penny. Their simple message worked and tea bags began to dominate the tea market. Tea bags may have changed over the years – in 1989 Tetley launched their round tea bag, while in 1997 PG Tips introduced their pyramid variety – but by 2007 they made up ninety-six per cent of the British market, with tea bags being cited as one of the top things that British holiday makers are most likely to pack in their luggage.

A storeroom containing boxes of Tetley tea bags.

Expensive tastes

If you've ever moaned about the price of your favourite tea bags going up, then consider that £7,500 is the highest price ever paid for a tea bag. This wasn't just any old bag, it was one commissioned to celebrate PG Tips' seventy-fifth anniversary. The luxury jewellery retailer and design company Boodles were tasked with creating a tea bag studded with 280 diamonds and filled with Silver Tips Imperial Tea from the Makibari Estate: the most expensive Darjeeling tea in the world. Meanwhile, one of the world's most expensive teas is panda tea, which comes from bushes that are fertilised with panda droppings and will set you back an eye-watering £35,000 per kg. However, if your budget is limitless then you may want to indulge in a pot of Da-Hong Pao, meaning Big Red Robe, which is considered the king of Chinese teas. A legendary tea with countless medicinal properties, it may do your health good but would be detrimental to your bank balance as it is the world's most expensive tea at £600,000 per kg. Perhaps it's not surprising that it doesn't come in a bag.

While some still maintain that loose leaf tea is superior to the tea bag, regardless of its shape, it has to be said that modern tea drinking has given us several of its most identifiable advertisements, from the cuddly Tetley Tea Folk to the PG Tips chimpanzees. Perhaps these were all amusing distractions to keep us laughing and buying tea without considering its origins and its true cost.

PG Tips' anniversary diamond studded teabag.

Chapter 8

The Tainted Tea of Lost Assam

As the modish and the elite enjoyed the sensory delights of tea outdoors in London's tea gardens, the tea gardens of Assam were growing the plants for profit and certainly not pleasure. The tea gardens of Assam were plantations dedicated to commercial tea growing. No flowered walks, shaded arbors or entertainment would be extended to those who trod these tea gardens: hard work and punishing conditions were the order of the day.

As the British press excitedly wrote about the British 'discovery' of tea in Assam, hopeful expectations of magnificent profits were nurtured. The excitement was further fuelled by the much publicised first auction of Assam tea and the enthusiastic reviews it received.

Botanists had believed that China was the native home of tea and the discovery that the teaplant, *Camellia sinensis*, was indigenous to Upper Assam was an exciting revelation. There was a real buzz surrounding the discovery as Britain contemplated that it could break free from her troubled and expensive relationship with China. It was considered that young imperial entrepreneurs may be able to embrace 'the opportunity of becoming partakers of that civilization, that innocent commerce, that knowledge and that faith with which it has pleased a gracious Providence to bless our own country.'[3] The plan was to mobilise the local population to work in the new tea gardens and it was optimistically predicted that the local labour force would embrace this new opportunity.

Within a decade of the first London sale of Assam tea in 1839, the riverboats on Assam's Brahmaputra river were full of young, ambitious British men looking to make their fortune. Filled with excitement over building lives as tea planters and dealers, they brought their 'essentials' from home, which included golf clubs and pedigree dogs. The Cornishman Albert Congdon of Duloe was typical of the adventurers who arrived in India in the nineteenth century to develop these new plantations. Aged eighteen and full of ambition, Congdon sailed to Calcutta in 1861 with Captain Rogers RN, who already owned estates in Assam. Congdon was taken on as manager of the Assam Tea Company at Burdwar, in the Ganhati district, and eventually acquired 800 acres of tea-growing country, employing some 2,000 pickers. In the 1880s Congdon shows up in Cornish trade directories listed either as a 'tea planter and importer' or a 'tea planter and dealer'.

It was economics, not romance, that brought the planters to Assam and, while fortunes were made, children born and families raised, the life of tea planters was far from quixotic, for while the warm and humid conditions were ideal for growing tea, they also provided the perfect breeding ground for pests and disease. There were also labour issues. The profitability of the private tea enterprise in Assam, and its ability to compete with Chinese tea, centered upon securing a reliable workforce.

The Assamese did not readily take to the roles offered in the tea gardens and colonial officials soon condemned the local peasants as the epitome of the 'lazy native'. Indeed, the reluctance of the Assamese to engage in the work and accept the conditions was conveniently blamed on 'opium mania', which was singled out as the prime reason for the decline of Assamese society. The influential tea planter, Robert Bruce, declared, "Opium mania, that dreadful plague which has depopulated this beautiful country, turned it into a land of wild beasts, with which it is overrun, and has degenerated the Assamese, from a fine race of people, to the most abject, servile, crafty, and demoralized race in India.'[4]

The solution being proffered was to simply import workers. This would bring its own set of problems, but none of these operational setbacks could dampen the confidence surrounding the 'discovery' of tea in Assam. Soon British planters bypassed local workers and came to rely on misplaced migrants. From the 1860s until the 1920s plantations in remote Assam recruited labourers from different parts of British India via a penal and indentured labour regime. Tea plantation workers became known as 'coolies'. The colonial master passed numerous laws to facilitate recruitment and control of Assam's migrant labour force, beginning with the 1863 Transport of Native Labourers Act. Men, women and children were sent from central India – a long and treacherous journey by steamer, road and, later, railway – into the jungles and gardens of Upper Assam. Many did not survive the journey and those that did would face the peril of atrocious working and living conditions.

Bourne and Shepherd, Calcutta

An example of a tea garden in Assam.

The demands for Assam tea continued to increase and the focus of the British government was on securing a workforce to supply the needs of the nation.

While the tea plantations were portrayed as being the land of plenty, there were many pests in this garden of paradise. The red spider mite was a major problem. The nymph and adult mites were spread by wind, animals, birds and by labourers' clothing and tea baskets. More worrying, though, than the red spider mite was the crippling blister blight, a fungal disease that struck hard in April and May of 1906. The tea planters' lack of experience and necessary horticultural training and expertise to deal with the persistence of pests, and the region's erratic rainfall, posed an extreme challenge to the crop's cultivation in nineteenth-century Assam.

As tea planters battled to manage tea pests they also had to manage the issues of labour resistance. It wasn't just issues relating to violence and aggression, or the refusal to work that tea planters needed to manage, they also had problems in using animal bone fertilizers. The caste restrictions forbade the use of animal ash, as it was considered an unacceptable pollutant. This caused disruption to the fertilisation of the crops and the operation was only able to continue properly once

FARMERS · IN · ASSAM
HAVE · THEIR · OWN
TIME · ZONE · CALLED
TEA · GARDEN · TIME

Tea Garden Time in Assam.

the planters started to hire labourers from lower castes, whose social position allowed them to handle animal ash.

Death from working in the tea gardens was a frequent occurrence and a likely prospect for tea workers in Assam. While the tea planters' profits flourished in the subtropical surroundings the conditions for the workers were less than healthy. The enchanting, romantic images of tea pickers that the British saw at home were a far cry from the unsanitary conditions that the workers were made to endure. The plantations were without latrines or adequate clean water and workers were forced to defecate in the tea bushes.

The British were developing a thirst for Assam tea, but the plantations were gaining a bad reputation for the high sickness and mortality rates among their workers, who perished as a result of poverty, malnourishment, and a lack of basic sanitation and healthcare facilities. Diseases and infections such as cholera, malaria, kala-azar (black fever), anemia, dysentery and dropsy, diarrhea and other infections were rife.

In 1877 DeRenzy took charge as Assam's Sanitary Commissioner and set to work immediately to demonstrate that the lack of adequate clean drinking water aboard the steamers, at labour depots and at camps, was the source of the cholera problem. In 1878 he wrote that there was only one tap supplying clean water to 400-500 labourers, meaning that they frequently resorted to using contaminated water supplies.

As the causes of cholera were debated, Kala-Azar claimed the lives of many tea workers. Meanwhile, Ancylostomiasis, a hookworm infection that attacks the intestines and leads to anemia, was a common problem. This condition was caused by skin exposure to larvae in soil contaminated by animal and human feces. The lack of latrines and basic sanitation was costing lives, but improved sanitation and malarial control continued to remain a non-priority. They were handled in a non-systematic manner, resulting in a continuous rise in mortality rates.

The British Medical Association drew strong links between human mismanagement and malaria in Assam. Addressing the Seventh Congress of the Far Eastern Association of Tropical Medicines and Hygiene in Calcutta, in December 1927, Ramsay warned, 'Truly, the cost of appropriate anti-malaria measures is trivial compared with the economic loss caused by this disease apart from the terrible wastage of life, ill-health and misery it creates.'[5]

The living and working conditions of the migrant tea workers were very different from the 'prosperity and peace' that London's press described. They endured squalid accommodation conditions, starvation wages, a harsh work regime and worse. There were practices of sexual exploitation, flogging for disobedience and various torture methods – including rubbing pepper into the genitals of female coolies – all of which were testimony to the contempt and dehumanisation shown to the tea workers by their bosses, who had, in effect, demoted the 'coolie' to the status of animal.

For many workers, the tea gardens of Assam were a living hell. Indentured labourers were subjected to almost semi-feudal oppression. They were under constant supervision and beatings were a part of their daily lives. Mixed-race and illegitimate children told of other exploitations these workers endured at the hands of the white tea masters, while the low birth and infant survival rates, and the high numbers of abortions among coolie women, became an acute concern only in the twentieth century.[6]

Tea cultivation in Assam had become synonymous with disease and death. Inadequate food, appalling living and working conditions and the spread of disease all led to high mortality rates. Assam's plantations were governed by profit and though laws that governed labour immigration and sanitary welfare were in place, all other considerations were secondary. The tea planters were thriving on their growing profits, their workers were experiencing low wages, malnourishment and a harsh regime.

The tea industry in Assam experienced increasing demands and the central importance of the Assam tea industry meant that the key focus of the government was to legalise the import of labour in order to continue maximum tea production and harvesting. When reports of abuse in the tea gardens became known and raised protests from officials, missionaries and the public in recruiting areas, the government averted its attention, putting profits first.

In 1888 a Bengal government official was appalled to learn of a tea planter organising a polyandrous marriage between seasoned coolies whose contracts had expired five times. Also distressing was the news that a single woman had been imported under the act. In return for the marital union, each man had agreed to re-engage in the same garden for a five-year period. The official noted, 'The disposal in marriage of all imported female coolies is considered as a matter entirely within the jurisdiction of the manager.'[7]

From the outset of their recruitment into the Assam tea gardens, coolies were often exploited and deceived by underhand recruiters

Tea pickers harvest the crop in Assam. Their living and working conditions were very different to those described to the wider world via propaganda.

and employers. Stories about what was going on circulated, as families often never saw those who left to work in the tea gardens ever again.

While abduction was practiced by some unscrupulous recruiters, the move to Assam was only considered a viable option for the poorest in society who had no choice. Sadly, what was seen as a means to an end often spelled the point of no return. Even once the contract time expired, coolies often had no means to return home. Stories of contract renewal under duress and of individuals being manipulated were rife. Assam became a place from which people never returned. Families of those who never returned suspected foul play; there were even rumours circulating of coolies being boiled down for oil[8], but such speculation could not hide the startling truth of sickness, abuse and death.

The perceptions and fears about Assam's tea gardens were reflected in oral traditions and folk songs. An Assamese song focuses on the dialogue between two lovers, where the man wants to go and work in an Assam tea garden to earn money, while his beloved pleads with him not to go to a place where 'there is not one bit of happiness'. The song's subsequent lines disdainfully depict a coolie woman in lustful union with white men.[9]

Tea planters were constantly under pressure to increase production. Financial bonuses for successfully reaching targets were offered alongside penalties and the threat of unemployment for failure, both of which drove the tough management of the labour force.

But while profits grew from 1890 onwards, reports of violence against coolies were being noted in the annual labour reports. A case was reported in 1890 of a coolie dying from excessive beating by a manager in Lakhimphur. At his trial the manager received a small fine and was free to return to manage his labour force. In 1899 in Rangliting tea garden of Lakhimpur district a young labourer was whipped and beaten to death. A police report was filed, but the guilty planters received only nominal fines.[10]

The tea gardens of Assam had been sold as those of hope, but had turned out to yield only despair for those who worked on them. The land of hope, security and opportunity was an illusion and coolies were entrapped into hardship and legalised slavery. Images at home in Britain unabashedly celebrated the 'joy' workers experienced in plucking tea leaves by creating an illusion that tea picking was a genteel art akin to picking wild flowers. These romantic perceptions were frequently employed in advertising but they hid the sheer intensity of the work and the terrible hardships that the tea pluckers faced.

Chapter 9

Tea in British Culture: Changing Customs and Rituals

Tea comes in all manner of styles: some people favour the dunk-and-go tea bag style of tea making, while others like big stewing pots of the stuff; some must have it brewed in a special cup while others are happy to drink from a chipped mug. There are debates galore about what makes a good cup of tea, and whether you prefer a builder's brew or a delicate cup of green tea, up and down the country kitchen cupboards are home to boxes of tea and jars of tea bags.

Our lives are awash with tea and the drink is surrounded by controversies, such as whether milk should be added first or last, which always fuels furious debates. How to make tea is often the subject of heated arguments, with everyone having their own particular set of golden rules.

Brewing your perfect cuppa at home is all well and good, but tea is not just the drink of break times and breakfast: it has an important social role to play. By the turn of the nineteenth century, tea had become an important part of daily life and its associated rituals and functions were distinctly British. By 1800 the British had made tea into the national beverage with its unique accoutrements and customs. From teapots, to sugar tongs and full china tea services, the equipage we have employed to sup this much-revered hot beverage is perhaps one of the most visible marks of British influence on tea.

The Chinese sent some of their teapots with the first shipments of tea in the 1600s, to be used as ballast and then sold as an exotic curiosity. These pots were made of heavy, unglazed ceramic and though the concept of the teapot was popular, the British began to adapt the designs and English potters made their first attempts to copy them in local clay. The British requirements for a teapot were exacting: it needed to be large enough to hold several cups of tea but not too heavy to lift;

it needed to balance well so as not to tip; it needed to pour well; and it needed to be easy to clean.

The basic design of the teapot remained the same across the classes with only the amount of decoration altering the value of the vessel. In 1698 Celia Fiennes, in her travel diary *The Journeys of Celia Fiennes*, describes how she 'went to this Newcastle in Staffordshire to see them making the fine tea-potts, cups and saucers of fine red earth, in imitation and as curious as that which comes from china.'

During the second half of the seventeenth century, European potters struggled to emulate the Chinese in their creation of fine porcelain teapots and only managed to produce a type of earthenware with a glaze, and later stoneware pots of inferior quality. The majority of tea ware being produced in England during the eighteenth century was soft-paste porcelain with a glass compound mixed into it. Although the resulting pieces had a reasonably hard finish, they were unsatisfactory and frequently lost their shape during the firing process. Like our cultivation of tea, our production of teaware took time to develop and shape into a mark of British life.

As Britain began to industrialise in the early eighteenth century and the demand for teaware increased, the Staffordshire potteries were given a huge boost. Enterprising potters developed their own range of decorative effects in an attempt to copy Chinese porcelain and its complex designs. However, there was a problem. Many of the glazes contained lead, which was fused inside the glaze during the firing process. If the glazes were not properly formulated, applied and fired, it was possible for them to leach into food or drink, which was especially problematic with hot, acidic tea. Those at most risk from lead poisoning, however, were not those serving the tea, but those workmen and women who were employed as dippers in the pottery industry and who were exposed to the lead oxide and lead carbonate in the glazes. Lead poisoning was a serious problem among dippers and their assistants in North Staffordshire, which was the manufacturing centre of earthenware and china in Britain. Lead normally builds up in the system over time and as it accumulates it begins to cause serious health problems. The pottery dippers were exposed daily to large amounts of lead and this caused colic, convulsions, paralysis of limbs, blindness and general emaciation. Female lead workers suffered excessively from abortions and miscarriages, and many of their infants died of fits. Ladies of leisure, meanwhile, continued in ignorance to sip their tea from delicate, lead-glazed tea cups as manufacturers tried to

A Staffordshire teapot, c. 1800, with lead-glazed redware.

find methods of glazing their products without lead or with lower lead content glazes.

Teapots were not the only aspect of the equipage to receive British modifications. The paraphernalia used to accompany the serving and drinking of tea conveyed the image of British social gentility and was the height of refinement. The ritual of brewing and serving tea was steeped in manners and etiquette, and it was considered crucial that the best tools for the job were made available.

Basic pieces in the set included the teapot, tea cups, saucers, sugar and cream bowls, sugar tongs, spoons and kettles. The first ever silver tea pot was made in England and was a gift to the East India Company from Baron George Berkeley. The task of producing silverware was challenging until the invention of metal rolling in a mill in the late 1600s, which made production quicker, easier and cheaper. Silver tea- and tableware became more readily available and by the beginning of the eighteenth century silver pots came in a variety of shapes, sizes and styles. Though silver teapots and tableware were prized for their beauty, many considered the china or earthenware teapot to be superior for the purpose of brewing tea. In *The Gracious Hostess* (1923) Thompson Lutes asserts that 'In making tea in a pot, china or earthenware is preferable. Silver keeps hot longer, but the flavour does not seem quite so delicate.'

Throughout the nineteenth century, society ladies did their very best to make sure that their tea party was as elegant and as stylish as those hosted by their friends. Books of etiquette were invaluable in giving careful instructions on how to lay out the table and how to conduct the art of taking tea properly. In Marie Bayard's *Hints on Etiquette* (1884), she directed, 'When an afternoon "'reception'" or party is given, and the table is to be arranged in the drawing room, it is usual to lay it on a large table in a corner of the room, spread with a cloth, tray, teapot, urn or spirit kettle, cakes, bread-and-butter, and a sufficient quantity of cups and saucers.' The table sounds familiar even for today's afternoon teas and perhaps the only change over time is that the list of equipment used for the serving of tea in formal situations has reduced.

As time progressed, tea ceremonies became more complex and the refinement of tea sets and other tea-related equipment took place. Items used to serve and brew tea were not used for other purposes, but reserved solely for the art of tea, allowing the taking of tea its unique place in the world of luxury goods. This fashion also allowed the wealthy to indulge themselves in ever-more charming, elegant, exclusive and expensive teaware.

Though the dawn of the British tea industry was the 1830s, British silversmiths and potters had started their tea-based industries much earlier. While we had looked to China for tea-taking inspiration, their tea equipment did not need to reflect the British style of taking tea: there were no cream jugs, sugar bowls, saucers or tongs. These items were needed to fulfill very British needs, and their creation added another exclusively British influence, thus elevating its status. In China, tea was taken without milk or sugar, but the British, being great culinary borrowers, had taken tea and transformed it into a very British institution.

The creation of these uniquely British tea accoutrements helped it gain acceptance in more refined social circles and the rituals associated with taking tea at the beginning of the nineteenth century also became very British. From the very earliest years of tea drinking in Britain, sugar had been added to tea and beautiful silver spoons for stirring sugar became a crucial ingredient in the process. Such accoutrements were the height of fashion, and were expensive. It is, therefore, not surprising that, in the seventeenth century, the London newspaper *Mercurius Politicus* includes silver spoons in a list of stolen property. The various spoons listed included 'wrought' spoons in 1685, 'small gilt' spoons in 1686, those 'with knobs' in 1697, and a 'long tea spoon' in 1697. In 1685, the *London Gazette* records the theft of 'six little wrought silver teaspoons and one tea pot', and in 1686 it makes reference to the theft of 'three small gilt tea spoons'.

As the porcelain bowls from which tea was drunk were dainty, the spoons were also small, and they remained of petite proportions until the late eighteenth century when they almost doubled in size, before reducing again in the 1870s. Saucers were also quite small and this called for special dishes to be made to place teaspoons and sugar-nippers on while not in use. This practice became obsolete from around 1760 onwards as cups and saucers grew larger and teaspoons could be placed on the saucer, once used.

The tea bowl and dish was gradually replaced by the cup. This was done by modifying the handle found on the English posset cup to suit the Oriental tea bowl. The posset cup was designed to hold the eponymous hot drink, which contained warmed milk, wine, spirits, spices and sugar. Posset cups were designed with a handle on each side to allow the cup to be easily held without burning fingers. The early English tea cups added a small handle to the side of the Oriental tea bowl, although the European manufacturers produced tea bowls with and without handles and this practice continued well into the nineteenth century. By the early nineteenth century all major British potteries were producing a good selection of tea cups, and tea sets were now beginning to take shape.

Tea has been subjected to strict etiquette rules and superstitions almost from the moment it was integrated into British culture. The correct use of the cup and saucer follows slightly different etiquette rules depending on the situation in which it is being used. If a tea party is taking place around a high table, such as a dining table, then it is quite correct to remove the cup for drinking and leave the saucer in place on the table. However, if tea is served from a low table, then it is *de rigeur* to lift both cup and saucer together before raising the

An illustration taken from *The Ladies Home Journal*, titled Tea with Mr. Rochester, by Coby Whitmore. When it came to taking tea, elegance was expected.

cup to the lips to drink from. In this instance the saucer should remain balanced in the left hand while the cup is raised to the lips in the right hand. The most important rule of etiquette when handling a cup and saucer is to remain elegant and graceful.

If you wish to avoid a *faux pas* you might want to observe some of the superstitions associated with tea before you pour a cup, especially if you like your brew to be enjoyed without scandal:

- Stirring the tea in the pot anti-clockwise will stir up trouble
- Spilling a little tea while making it is a lucky omen.
- Bubbles on the surface of your tea denote kisses or money.
- If two women pour from the same pot, one of them will have a baby within the year
- If you put milk in your tea before sugar you risk crossing the path of love; you may never marry.
- If you make tea that is stronger than usual, this indicates the beginning of a new friendship. Make your tea weaker and you will lose a friend.
- If two teaspoons are accidentally placed together on a saucer, this points to the occasion of a wedding or a new pregnancy.

While tea superstitions and etiquette continued to develop, so too did the demand for tea pots for all types and classes, as those of lesser means attempted to imitate the tea rituals of the upper classes. For those who could not afford silver teapots, pewter teapots were the answer. Pewter is an alloy of tin, and contains lead, antimony, (a close relation of arsenic) bismuth and copper. As already discussed, lead accumulates in the soft tissue and bones, damaging the nervous system and interfering with the production of red blood cells. Up until 1800 pewter was familiar and widespread; the equivalent of today's plastic. Any utensil that did not come into direct contact with a flame, such as plates, teapots, flagons, jugs, bowls and pots, would commonly be made from pewter. In the 1770s a new type of pewter was invented. This was laced with extra antimony and was known as Britannia Metal. It was sold highly polished and unashamedly aped silver. As it was harder than the original pewter, it enabled it to be made into thin sheets for stamping into moulds, or spun (forced into shape while spinning on a wooden chuck on a lathe). It was a popular choice with middle classes as it looked good on tea tables. Britannia Metal wares were manufactured in various ornate designs and mass produced at a fraction of the price of pieces fashioned from other metals: indeed, they were about one thirtieth of the price of silver.

As lead was a major element in the production of early pewter, it caused many illnesses by leaching into food and tea. Even small amounts of the acids found naturally in some foods and drinks caused the pewter to pit or discolour, while the lead naturally leached. Pewter was not only attractive but also dangerous. As taking tea became a more genteel and fashionable pastime, so did women's exposure to lead increase dramatically. In the eighteenth century fashionable women already mixed lead with vinegar to make ceruse, which helped them achieve a 'porcelain' complexion and visually smooth out the facial appearance. Lead was even used as a spermicide for birth control. As fashionable ladies sat with their painted faces, drinking adulterated tea from their stylish teapots that were leaching lead, they were slowly poisoning themselves, and in the meantime suffering side effects such as greying hair, dry skin, severe abdominal pain and constipation.

During the 1830s taking tea had become so popular and such an accepted practice, that business entrepreneurs soon saw a gap in the market for catering outlets that exuded respectability and sold tea. A great many tea rooms opened and though they may sound similar to the coffee-houses of the seventeenth century, they were different in that these new businesses catered to the needs of ordinary people, not just wealthy men, and were frequented by women. From the 1880s, tea rooms and tea shops became popular and fashionable with women who embraced the opportunity to enjoy a refreshment in a socially acceptable environment that afforded them the chance to meet, chat and relax, without the need to be accompanied by a man.

Later in the nineteenth century going out to a tea shop became a popular pastime for women. It even extended to women of the lower classes, such as those in service who would visit on their afternoon off. Despite the rise of the tea room, however, tea remained a beverage that was mostly drunk at home. Enjoyed at breakfast by all social classes, it not only became the staple of the English morning ritual but also a refreshment that was enjoyed throughout the day.

Rich or poor, tea was the drink that extended its warm comfort to everyone. In the nineteenth century Charles Dickens refers to tea drinking among the working classes, and through the eyes of Pip, the protagonist of *Great Expectations*, we can sense Dickens' affection for it:

We returned into the Castle, where we found Miss Skiffins preparing tea. The responsibility of making toast was delegated to the Aged [an elderly man] ... The Aged prepared such a haystack of buttered toast, that I could scarcely see him over it ... while Miss Skiffins prepared such a jorum of tea, that the pig in the back premises became strongly excited ... We ate the whole of the toast, and drank tea in proportion, and it was delightful to see how warm and greasy we all got after it.

Whilst the poor grasped a cup of tea to revive them from their hard day's labour and stave off the cold and hunger, the rich were enjoying afternoon tea in much the same way that ladies of the seventeenth century enjoyed their tea parties.

Tradition has it that afternoon tea was 'invented' by Anna Maria, the wife of the seventh Duke of Bedford, who, in 1841, started drinking tea and

With the end of the working day came tea time. This painting, circa 1800, depicts the longed-for moment of return.

having a bite to eat in the mid-afternoon, to tide her over during the long gaps between meals. This swiftly developed into a social occasion, and soon the duchess was inviting guests to join her for afternoon tea. By the 1860s the fashion for afternoon tea had become widespread. They were such elegant affairs that they required yet more teaware and ever more elaborate tea sets.

A certain etiquette was again applied and guides on how to conduct oneself when attending and hosting such events were soon in circulation. The hostess would pour the tea, but it was the responsibility of the men to hand the cups round. If there were no men present, this job fell to the daughters of the hostess or other young women present. These fashionable affairs gave the perfect opportunity for the wearing of tea gowns, sometimes even without the need to wear gloves, thus extending even more liberty to fashionable society women as they enjoyed their tea.

By the beginning of the twentieth century there could be no doubt about the importance of tea to the British people. This was acknowledged by the government during the First World War. Tea was not initially rationed, but tea prices began to rise as a result of ships being sunk by German submarines, and so the government swiftly took over the importation of tea and controlled prices. During the Second World War the government took even more drastic action to safeguard the availability of this essential morale booster. Just two days after war broke out, the government took control of all tea stocks and ordered that the vast reserves stored in London must be dispersed to warehouses outside the capital in case of bombing. When enemy blockades prevented ships from getting through, the Ministry of Food introduced a ration of 2oz of tea per person per week for those over the age of five. This was not a lot of tea for a tea-addicted nation, however. The ration would have yielded enough for two or three cups a day of rather weak tea. But there was extra tea for those in the armed forces, and on the domestic front for those in vital jobs such as firemen and steel workers. Tea was also sent in Red Cross parcels to British prisoners of war abroad. The tea-loving housewives eked out tea rations and had to continue doing so until tea came 'off the ration' in October 1952.

Despite the rationing of tea, the British love affair with the beverage remained strong. In January 1946 the author and journalist George Orwell published an essay called 'A Nice Cup of Tea' in the *Evening Standard* newspaper, calling tea 'one of the main stays of civilsation in this country,' and listing his eleven 'golden rules' for tea making.

A drawing by Kate Greenaway, depicting the elegant ritual of afternoon tea.

Orwell acknowledged the controversial nature of some of them – such as his insistence that the tea should be poured and then the milk added, and that tea should always be drunk without sugar – but he also offered sensible advice to make the 2oz ration go as far as possible, such as using water that is still at the point of boiling, in order to make the strongest brew from the least tea.

Certainly for much of the twentieth century, methods of preparing tea were still the subject of some snobbery. In a letter to Nancy Mitford, the author Evelyn Waugh mentions a mutual friend who uses the expression 'rather milk in first' to express condemnation of those lower down the social scale.

Tea has, for centuries, been at the very heart of social life in Britain. Drinking tea is an important part of our daily lives and it is presented as a cure-all for many of life's ills. No matter how tragic the event unfolding may be, 'let's have a nice cup of tea' is what people say, whether your pet goldfish has died, or you've been served with divorce papers, lost your job, or been given a terminal diagnosis. Tea is not just the rather twee

Crew aboard a minesweeper enjoy a nice cup of tea, in March 1943.

height of Englishness, it is also the most basic solution to any problem: the equivalent to a hug or a sticking plaster in a mug.

Britain's national beverage, however, may not always be the remedy to your ills; it may actually be the cause of your undoing. Tea has a wicked past and throughout history there have been those who have been, quite literally, dying for a cup of tea. Death by tea is not just the stuff of murder mystery novels or television dramas, where silver-haired lady detectives uncover a plot to poison a wealthy relative. Throughout history there have been real-life murderers who have used tea as a way to entice their victims to their grim fate.

Graham Young had a preoccupation with death. From a young age he had a fascination with poisons and his devotion to the study of chemicals got him dubbed the 'mad professor' by his peers at school. Young became so well versed in toxicology that he was able to acquire quantities of poisonous chemicals at the age of thirteen by convincing chemists that he was older than his actual years and that the use was purely for the purposes of study. When Young became tired of the lab experiments he decided to use real, live people as guinea pigs. In order to conduct his toxic experiments he would serve tea laced with poisonous concoctions to his family and schoolmates. In 1961 his stepmother, Molly, started developing bad stomach cramps, while Young's father and older sister began to suffer similar pains soon after. A classmate named Christopher Williams also developed similar symptoms. At first no one suspected Young, and the symptoms of his friend and family were attributed to a stomach bug.

However, things were about to get worse. Young's sister, Winifred, once again became extremely ill while on her way to work. She was taken to the hospital, where doctors discovered belladonna, the extract of deadly nightshade, in her system. She survived, but Young's family were becoming suspicious of his involvement in their mysterious ailments.

On 21 April 1962, Young's stepmother was rushed to hospital in excruciating pain. She died later that night. It was found out that Young had slowly been poisoning his stepmother's tea with antimony, to which she developed a tolerance. However, the night before her death, he switched to thallium in order to quicken the process of death.

On 23 May 1962, Graham Young was arrested. He confessed to the murder of his stepmother as well as the poisoning of his other family members. In his interviews with the police, he boasted of his considerable knowledge of toxicology. As to poisoning his victims, he told Chief Superintendent Harvey: 'I had ceased to see them as people … they became guinea pigs.' Despite his confessions, however, there was no evidence to substantiate Young's claims as Molly Young's body had been cremated. No murder charge was brought against him; instead, he was placed in Broadmoor maximum security hospital. At just fourteen years of age he was their youngest inmate. By June 1970 his doctors at the hospital deemed him 'cured' and he was released.

Once released, Young found himself a perfect job working at John Hadland Laboratories in Bovingdon, in Hertfordshire, where they manufactured infra-red lenses for military equipment, using thallium. Though his employers were aware of his psychiatric stay, they didn't know the reason behind it, so when Young asked to make tea for his co-workers they gratefully accepted his kind offer.

Soon, illness swept through the lab and it was put down to a stomach bug. Young's colleagues continued to drink the tea he made them, without them knowing of his disturbing history. They had no reason to suspect that Young, who was always quick to suggest making tea for everyone, was actually poisoning them.

It wasn't long before the suspected stomach bug led to deaths. Bob Egle was the first to die, becoming completely debilitated before his eventual passing on 7 July 1971, closely followed by Fred Biggs. By this stage nearly seventy employees had experienced similar symptoms of the two deceased men.

Still the mysterious deaths and illnesses were not thought to be connected to Young. It wasn't until a conversation he had with a staff doctor that Young's in-depth knowledge of toxicology was revealed. He asked the doctor why thallium poisoning wasn't being considered as the cause since it was used on site. It was this conversation that finally gave cause for concern and the police were alerted.

An investigative team found Young's diary, in which he described with scientific detachment the experiments and how he had poisoned his co-workers. He was also found with thallium in his possession. Young was sentenced to life imprisonment in June 1972, and in 1990 he was found dead in his cell. The official cause of death was recorded as a heart attack, but speculation was that he poisoned himself.

Though Young is long gone, in recent years he inspired a sixteen-year-old girl in Japan to lace her mother's tea and food with thallium. She kept records of her mother's decline and even tried to poison her mother's tea while she was in hospital and take photographs of her while she was in a coma. She admitted poisoning her mother and expressed an admiration for Graham Young after reading his biography. In her room, investigators found several animal parts that she had dissected and preserved in formalin, including the severed head of a cat, alongside her chilling notes in which she recorded: 'To kill a living creature. The moment of sticking a knife into something. The little sigh. I find it comforting.'

Tea is not always the vehicle of murder but sometimes the refreshment taken afterwards. John Haigh was the serial killer who murdered the rich in order to fuel a life of luxury. Through the murder of his rich victims he was able to live in an expensive London hotel and have his suits made in Saville Row, along with all the other trappings of a wealthy life. If you were rich and accepted his offer of afternoon tea or a drink in his hotel room the chances were you ended up being shot and your body dumped into a vat of sulphuric acid. But he'd always make time for a cuppa afterwards.

His sixth and final victim was a wealthy widow, Mrs Olive Durand-Deacon, whom he had befriended. When Mrs Durand-Deacon went missing, the police visited the hotel where she had been staying and questioned Haigh. His spry manner struck discord with one of the police officers and led to investigations that revealed Haigh had sold off his victim's jewellery. A search of a workshop and yard that Haigh rented revealed the presence of a couple of human gallstones and a set of false teeth; all that remained of Mrs Durand-Deacon. A thorough investigation of the site revealed the grisly presence of 28lb of human body fat and part of a human foot. Haigh confessed to the murder and to five others, and explained that he shot his victims first, before plunging their bodies into a metal drum filled with acid. After a couple of days, he would pour the liquefied remains down the drain. His crimes spanned the period between 1944 and 1949. In his confession he said that in the case of Mrs Durand-Deacon he had found time between the shooting and acid treatment for a cup of tea and a fried egg on toast at the local café, proving that murder is thirsty work and tea is suitable for all occasions.

The brutal killing of several prostitutes by two sailors became known as the 'Teapot Murders', though they didn't actually involve a teapot. It was due to the fact that the murders were committed on Lyons Street in Bootle, Liverpool, which was associated with the famous brand of tea during that period. The street name was further blackened by the vicious and cruel killing of Maggie Donoghue, who had her brains bashed out by a fireman, Jim McGuirk, in 1903, and the mysterious and callous killing of six-year-old Tommy Foy in 1908. Even the strongest cup of tea could not soothe away the chill of these killings.

There have been plenty of infamous teapot murderers, including Mary Ann Cotton, but there are also those who tried and failed in the attempt. In 1852 two women, Sarah Rimmer and Ann Rimmer, were charged at Liverpool Police Court with attempting to poison nineteen-year-old Elizabeth Rimmer, the daughter of the former. It was reported that, after drinking a cup of tea from a teapot that her mother and aunt had kept warm for her, she had noticed that it tasted unusually sweet. Upon drinking more tea her stomach and throat began to burn. In a previous argument her aunt and mother had threatened to poison her, and so, suspecting that she had now been poisoned by their tea, she took the remains of the pot to the druggist who analysed it and confirmed it contained the deadly poison, oxalic acid. The two women were sentenced to death and seemed indifferent to the judgment and unapologetic for their actions, but at least Elizabeth Rimmer was able to go home and enjoy a nice cup of tea.

Chapter 10

Witchcraft, Scrying and Sorcery

It isn't surprising to see tea feature in so many scandals and superstitions, given its central and long-standing function in British social life. There is no doubt that tea is magical stuff, capable of reviving weary souls and refreshing stagnant conversations. But aside from providing the key to a refreshing break, tea is actually believed to have qualities deeply rooted in magic lore. Wise women, alchemists and witches in folktales have all searched for the perfect brew to heal, to help and to achieve their every will. Tea magic is in fact an ancient and very powerful art that employs belief and divination.

Cunning women, kitchen witches and herbalists alike have all found wisdom in the use of herbs; from prosperity spells to those used to banish nightmares, tea leaves have appeared in a variety of concoctions.

A Spell to Banish Bad Dreams

To ensure good sleep, fill a pillow with dried tea leaves and lie on it at bedtime. Wise women believed they could banish negative thoughts, sleep disturbances and nightmares in this way, whilst simultaneously refreshing energies.

Perhaps it is needless to say that not all tea is considered equal when it comes to magical properties. Whilst most types of tea come from the leaves of *Camellia sinensis,* it is important to remember that different parts of the plant are used depending on the healing ritual at hand. Different varieties of the plant impart distinctive tastes, as well as varying healing properties. The alchemical properties of each type of tea are believed to differ in relation to growing conditions and the benefits of each type vary according to the season.

The Magical Qualities of Black Tea

Energy: Masculine
Planet: Mars
Element: Fire
Season: Winter

Black tea is created by fermented tea leaves. It is a type of tea that is more oxidized than green tea and is generally stronger and more intense in flavour than the less oxidized brews.

It's pretty well established that tea's flavonoids and anti-inflammatory compounds benefit the heart and that they may help prevent a range of health conditions including strokes. 'Magically' speaking, the properties of black tea are perhaps lesser known, however there is evidence of it having been used in spells to increase courage, to banish boredom, to stimulate the mind and to attract wealth.

Black Tea Instant Money Magic Spell

Hold a handful of black tea prior to brewing and visualize the flow of money, concentrating on riches coming to you easily, whilst reciting, "money come, money flow". When you feel ready, place the tea leaves into a teapot and brew as usual. Whilst drinking the resulting brew, imagine becoming wealthier and more financially independent.

The Magical Qualities of Green Tea

Energy: Masculine
Element: Fire
Planet: Mars
Season: Summer

As mentioned above, green tea is made from *Camellia sinensis* leaves that have not undergone the same withering and oxidation process used to make black tea. As such, it has a lighter, smoother flavour than its matured relative.

Green tea is richer in flavonoids and catechins and is considered to be beneficial in a variety of ways. It is incorporated in spells for health, longevity, love and intimacy, sexual energy, immortality, the banishment of negativity and the attraction of wealth.

Throughout history, both green and black teas have been mixed with other herbs, including mugwort and rose petals to create divination teas. Whilst folklore sees recipes for baldness featuring poultices made of used tealeaves, cowpats and the urine of animals, modern studies show green tea is particularly good for the hair. Rich in catechins which help to reduce dihydrotestosterone (DTH – responsible for hair loss), green tea can also improve scalp condition and fight dandruff.

Whilst some have met an unfortunate fate at the bottom of a tea cup, others have sought to weave magical tea spells to create the future they desire, leaving others to devote their time to looking for it in tea dregs. Today, tasseography or tea leaf reading tends to be associated with

An old fortune-teller is reading a young woman's fortune by looking at tea leaves at the bottom of a cup. Engraving by Sharpe after Crowley, 1842.

fairgrounds and side shows, however, it is an ancient Chinese practice that spread to Europe with Nomadic Gypsies in the 1800s.

Once an aristocratic beverage, tea became the drink of the masses. The culturally superstitious lower classes were quick to use tea leaves instead of other more cumbersome and often more dangerous methods of divination, such as molten metal (molybdomancy), hot wax (carromancy) or the entrails of animals (haruspicy). The eighteenth century book *Reading Tea Leaves* by A Highland Seer refers to generations of Scottish "spae wives" (from the Norse spa, meaning "prophecy") peering into tea cups in order to predict their fortunes.

There is more to tea-leaf reading than simply drinking a cup of tea and staring at the dregs. Traditionally the tea would be brewed and drunk with the intent of learning things to come. The tea would be poured from a pot into a tea cup without straining, leaving tea-leaf laden dregs after drinking. The cup would then be spun anti-clockwise with the left hand three times before the tea-cup was flipped upside-down into a saucer, revealing what the tea-leaves had to say. This was a popular form of prediction used throughout the generations, but it was in the Victorian era that tea-leaf reading reached its peak of popularity. The Victorians were fascinated by the occult, ideas of sorcery, fortune telling and also the process of self-analysis, something that gained popularity during this era due to the work of Sigmund Freud and Josef Breuer.

Scrying, palmistry, tasseography and other forms of fortune-telling reached great popularity during the nineteenth century. They were a fashionable form of entertainment and fascination, with husband divination games being a feature of Christmas and festive parties. Professional fortune tellers were employed to entertain visitors to the finest drawing rooms in London. In general, such activities were viewed as nothing more than rousing entertainment although there were those who had great belief in the powers of divination. A serious desire to learn the future or to contact the dead (coupled with a serious budget) gave rise to a seemingly endless parade of fraudsters and charlatans.

For the prosperous upper classes of society, fortune telling activities were delightful drawing room entertainments. However, for clairvoyants and fraudsters alike, these practices could end with the medium being prosecuted for fortune-telling under the Vagrancy Act.

Tea leaf reading was a popular subject for greeting cards throughout the twentieth century.

'....every person pretending or professing to tell fortunes, or using any subtle craft, means, or device, by palmistry or otherwise, to deceive and impose on any of his Majesty's subjects....shall be deemed a rogue and vagabond'.

[excerpt from The Vagrancy Act of 1824]

Mystics and fortune tellers were at constant risk of being sentenced to prison, hard labour, or deportation. If they were not tried and convicted under the Vagrancy Act, they could be found guilty under the Witchcraft Act of 1735. There is of course a sad possibility that some individuals, genuinely gifted with unusual powers of deep psychic intuition, suffered unnecessarily at the hands of these two acts. But, as fortune telling attracted such a plethora of scoundrels, many convictions were quite deservedly handed out. One such conviction was of Joseph Powell. In 1807, Powell was tried for fortune-telling under the Vagrancy Act. He was described in the court record as a "rogue and a vagabond," who had not only imposed himself on "credulous persons" and duped servants out of their "last shillings," but had also taken gross, lascivious advantage of women who had consulted him to find out whether they would ever be with child. Powell practiced his ruse through correspondence and was evidently a persuasive letter writer as the prosecutor in the case relates:

> *One of his letters in particular seems to have been addressed to a female, not of the lowest class, (who stated herself to be married, and who wished to be informed whether she should have any children) and the copy of this letter answers, that she is certainly destined to have children if she takes the means, but not by her husband; that it must be by some other person; that he shall be happy himself to be that person, and that he has no doubt their endeavors will be propitious to the object she has at heart. He then goes on to invite her to come the next day, when he promises to have his place clear, as well for comfort as safety.*

[Gurney, *Trial of J. Powell*, 3-4]
Powell charged anything from half a crown to five guineas for his services, but in the above instance the prosecutor states: "So strong was his amorous propensity on this occasion, that he tells the lady if she agrees to his proposal, that he will give her as much information as he should charge another person five guineas for, but that he will remit the five guineas in her case!" [Gurney, 5]

Not surprisingly, the crooked Mr Powell was sentenced to six months imprisonment. Meanwhile, the Witchcraft Act of 1735 made liable for punishment any person "pretending" to exercise or use any kind of witchcraft, sorcery, enchantment, or conjuration and this included telling fortunes. Under this act, many people were tried for palmistry, clairvoyance and tea-leaf reading. In 1914 the art of tea-leaf reading was to take centre stage in the trial of Aimee Henrietta Lake – the last woman in Guernsey to stand trial as a witch.

Before the Great War, Guernsey was an isolated and superstitious community with a strong belief in witchcraft and a fear of magical curses. It was a place where many things were considered unlucky; ledges were not built into chimney stacks, for example, so as to remove the possibility that witches might rest there on their travels. So, when PC Adams was called out in the early hours of the morning on 16 January 1914 following allegations of witchcraft practices, it was bound to send ripples throughout the superstitious community.

A local woman, Mrs Houtin, had banged on the doors of the office 'in an agitated state', pleading for police protection because 'a spell of witchcraft had been put on her' for non-payment of a £3 debt. Unless she paid immediately, it was warned, she would come to harm. As Mrs Houtin didn't have the money to service the debt, she feared an untimely death by black magic and was understandably hysterical.

In her statement to the police, Mrs Houtin explained that her husband had died unexpectedly the previous year and that she had recently had a bout of bad luck with her cattle inexplicably dying. This had caused her to seek the divinatory services of Mrs Aimee Lake. The police conducted a preliminary search of Mrs Houtin's property and discovered a box of powder in the outhouse and some charms for members of her family, which Houtin explained were supplied to her by Aimee Lake.

Aimee Lake was a mother of three and was carrying her absent husband's fourth child. Lacking sufficient marital maintenance, the former housekeeper made a living for herself and her children by tarot reading, telling fortunes through tea cup divination and explaining the significance of dreams, as well as dispensing charms made of harmless, everyday kitchen cupboard ingredients including flour, starch and baking powder, which were consequently labelled 'magic' powders.

Mrs Houtin explained how Aimee Lake had made some tea for herself and Mrs Houtin over which they had chatted. After drinking the tea, Aimee read the tea leaves in Mrs Houtin's cup, informing her that she was under a cursed spell – just as her late husband had been at the time of his death. Aimee then sold Mrs Houtin some 'magic' powders to burn and some to bury on her land. These 'charmed packets' were sold for the sum of £3 10 shillings.

On 29 January 1914, Aimee Lake stood in court before Bailiff William Carey and Mr G. E. Kinnersley accused of 'disorderly conduct and carrying on the trade of fortune-telling and witchcraft'. It was alleged that between 1913 and 1914, Mrs Lake had been operating as a intuitive advisor offering her skills in fortune telling and dream interpretation, practicing witchcraft in exchange for financial rewards.

Lake attempted to defend herself by saying that people came to her of their own free will and asked for her divinatory help. She denied that she was a witch and any allegations of intent to deceive, explaining that she simply tried to help those with troubles through the use of her special powders. However, by the time of Aimee's trial the 'special powders' had been analysed and were shown to contain baking powder, brown starch and a large amount of Brown and Polson's cornflour, from which blancmange was usually made. Thus the 'special powders' were dismissed as a device of mischief.

It is certain that Aimee Lake had not predicted her own fate in her teacup, for when she was convicted at Guernsey Royal Court of witchcraft she collapsed. Despite being five months pregnant and having other children to singularly care for, she was sentenced to the maximum-possible sentence for witchcraft: eight days in prison. Although she was frantic for the welfare of her children during her prison spell, it must be concluded that Aimee

Brown & Polson's famed and patented cornflour.

faired much better than a distant ancestor of hers, Alechette Queripel, who was branded a witch and consequently burned at the stake in 1598.

Whilst Aimee Lake's fortune did not lie in tasseography, traveling gypsies had long taken up the practice of tea-leaf reading, often calling door-to-door to offer their services. So popular were their talents that by the mid-1800s, the Roma had become part of the social scene, welcomed into both parlours and tea rooms to give readings for a fee or generous donation.

With tea-leaf reading becoming such a popular pastime and form of divination, it's perhaps not surprising that people were so eager to learn the art of tasseography themselves for personal prediction and entertainment purposes. The potteries offered a solution when they began making fortune telling cups. These mystically designed cups came with an instruction booklet and were decorated with symbols of the zodiac, playing cards or common symbols in tea-leaf reading. All the major potteries were creating these cups and the demand was high as wealthy Victorian ladies began to host social gatherings that centered around tea and its divining qualities.

Commonly spotted patterns in tea-leaf reading include anchors, circles, dogs and birds, interpreted variously depending on the surrounding shapes and white space in the tea cup. Those using commercially available fortune telling cups would no doubt have followed guidebooks offering fairly generic interpretations of the symbols that might appear at the bottom of a cup.

Tea-leaf reading faded as loose tea dwindled in popularity. However, the search for answers and meaning remains. As such, it is not surprising that tea-leaf reading still holds a fascination today.

Part of the ritual of this form of divination is to sit down and savour the tea. It offers an opportunity to relax and to gather your thoughts. If nothing else, it is a perfect excuse to rest and enjoy a good cup of Rosie-Lee.

For tea-leaf reading, you will need:

- Some loose leaf tea
- A teapot
- A cup and saucer (pale in colour and un-patterned on the inside so the leaves and shapes show up well)
- A relaxed frame of mind

Method:

Brew your tea in the teapot.

Pour yourself a cup - don't strain out the leaves, we will need these later! Enjoy your tea. Drink most of it, leaving the leaf fragments suspended in the last little sip of tea.

Hold the cup in your left hand. Think of a question and fix it in your mind. Swirl the tea dregs in your cup three times anti-clockwise.

Place the saucer on top of the cup, and flip the whole thing upside down so that the tea drains out into the saucer.

Turn over your cup. Look at where the leaves are, and at the patterns and shapes made. Your first thoughts on this really count, there is no right or wrong answer so trust your intuition.

Where a shape or pattern is in the cup indicates the 'when', as in the timescale of the event or happening. Objects closer to the rim are going to happen soon (the next few days), things nearer the base of the cup are further away in the future (generally, a cup shows you the next month).

Use your creativity when you are reading your cup. You are unlikely to get an arrangement of tea leaves that looks just like an aeroplane, so close one eye and squint a bit. Let your mind drift and wander, tip the cup this way and that and let your imagination run free.

Things to note before you read the leaves:

Bubbles on the surface of your tea mean that money is on its way.

If any tea leaves are floating on the surface, then visitors are imminent. The number of leaves shows how many days away they are.

If two teaspoons are accidentally placed on a saucer, then you can expect news of twins soon.

If a teaspoon is placed upside down onto a saucer, then you will hear news of the ill-health of a close relative.

If the question you seek the answer to relates to the prospect of marriage, then you may want to try this old gypsy fortune telling technique: take a teaspoon and balance it on the edge of your teacup, now carefully drip tea into the spoon, one drop at a time. Count the drips. Eventually the balance of the spoon will be broken. The number of drips it takes to upset the balance and topple the spoon is the number of years until a marriage will occur.

Tea Leaf Symbols and Their Meanings:

A

Abbey	– a sign of increasing prosperity and good fortune; you will gain much success in your life.
Ace of Clubs	– this signifies powerful forces are in play in relation to business, contracts and legal dealings.
Ace of Diamonds	– a change in financial fortunes.
Ace of Hearts	– shows affection and happiness in the home.
Ace of Spades	– sorrow, challenges and disruption.
Acorn	– this is a symbol of growing good fortune. Several acorns symbolise good fortune and improved circumstances, whereas an acorn near the handle of the cup indicates wealth coming your way, and towards the far side means possible financial aid through someone's help.

Aged Figure	– the symbol of an old man or woman represents a decline in your fortunes and that all your attention and focus will be required to keep afloat.
Aeroplane	– a journey or a promotion, you will rise in life.
Anchor	– a lucky sign, success in business or love. A sign that you will be establishing yourself and setting down roots.
Angel	– good news will appear soon!
Ant	– a symbol of hard work, industry, perseverance and determination. Success will come through your persistent efforts.
Apples	– you will have longevity.
Arrow	– bad news is on its way. If there are dots around the arrow the news may be connected with money.
Axe	– separation, estrangement or change lies ahead. A journey of change is about to commence.

B

Baby	– new beginnings.
Bag	– a warning of underhand dealings and plots being made against you.
Ball	– you will be the plaything of fortune and will encounter many ups and downs.
Basket	– if seen near a house this can mean an addition to your family is on the way. It can also mean that a gift is on its way to you.
Bat	– false friends; things are not as they seem.
Bear	– you will have to make a long journey soon and may need to overcome obstacles through strength and brute force.
Bee	– prosperity, acquisition of wealth through trade and a positive change in fortunes.
Ball	– your fortunes in life are going to bounce about both up and down.
Balloon	– your enthusiasm for something will float off into the clouds and disappear.
Banana skin	– you are unlucky in love. Try to accept it gracefully.
Bird	– good news is winging its way to you.

Butterfly	— brief pleasure and joy will come into your life, but may not last.
Bell	— a forthcoming announcement. Near the handle it signifies a particularly fortunate announcement, whereas an upside down bell signifies bad news and two bells signify marriage.
Besom (broom)	— scandals and rumors will be swept away. You are in a position to tidy up your life and sweep away problems.
Boat	— a possible journey or a visitor from afar.
Book	— an open book signifies news that will serve you well, whereas a closed book signifies the need for caution before action and for research.
Boot	— if the symbol of the boot is clear and well defined it is a sign of protection from danger, if it is rough and tattered it indicates disgrace and a fall from position.

C

Cage	— a symbol of marriage, if the symbol is clear and away from all other symbols it signifies a forthcoming marriage proposal.
Cake	— pleasure and cause for celebration.
Candle	— a sign of hope and good deeds. You have the opportunity to help others and better yourself.
Car	— wealth approaches, and visits from friends.
Castle	— an unexpected fortune or a legacy will arrive or else you will gain the favor of those in good positions of power.
Cat	— a false friend! Beware! In business this can signify underhand and crafty dealings. However, if the cat is curled up or resting it can mean home comforts.
Circle	— money or gifts are coming your way. An incomplete circle shows that an offer may change...
Clover	— luck, happiness and prosperity.
Coffin	— this does not necessarily spell death, but an end to a way of life or routine, such as a job or relationship. It can also spell business failure, loss or illness.
Coin	— prosperity or financial gain.

Cow	– a good omen, things you love will be near you.
Cradle	– new projects and beginnings, however if the cradle is broken it may spell trouble ahead.
Chair	– someone new is coming into your life...
Clouds	– trouble is on the way!
Crown	– your abilities will be recognized.
Cross	– a warning sign.

D

Dagger	– beware of danger.
Death	– this can be indicated in many ways including a skull or a black flag, it means the end to something. A dead person means unexpected change.
Deer	– good news from afar or the need to make a quick decision.
Devil or Demon	– be cautious of false advice.
Dog	– a good friend will support you.
Door	– opportunity is ripe.
Dragon	– great and sudden changes will occur.
Duck	– good news.

E

Eagle	– your fortunes will soar.
Egg	– a good omen of wholeness.
Elephant	– you will have good health.
Envelope	– unexpected news.
Explosion	– violent upsets and disruptions.
Eye	– a symbol of intelligence or a warning to take care in all business dealings - this can also be symbolised by optical glasses.

F

Feet	– you will be called upon to take a decisive step in some matter which may lead to a significant change in your life.
Fence	– minor setbacks occur which will not be permanent.
Ferns	– dignity, peace, and steadfast love.
Ferret	– jealousy and enmity are likely to cause you distress.

Ferry-Boat	– this symbol implies that difficulties will be smoothed away for you by the aid of good, true and useful friends.
Fish	– a symbol of great fortune, signifying increased prosperity.
Fist	– guard against impulses
Flag	– this is often a sign of danger or signifies the need for caution to be exercised. It can mean a call to duty or taking on more responsibility.
Flower	– happiness, admiration and success will be coming to you.
Fox	– treachery! And from a source you trust.
Frog	– you will have good luck and success at work.
Fruit	– an increase in abundance.

G

Gate	– if open it signifies opportunity, if closed it means barriers and obstacles ahead.
Ghost	– a threat of danger from an unexpected source.
Girl	– happiness and joy.
Glass (eye glass)	– you need to look at a troubling situation from another perspective.
Glass (drinking)	– a symbol of fragility; you lack strength and firmness.
Goat	– misfortune through being obstinate.
Grapes	– increased fortune with increased responsibility.
Grave	– news of a death.
Guitar	– happiness in love.

H

Hand	– somebody, somewhere, is trying to point something out to you.
Hare	– a need to be brave and assertive.
Harp	– harmony and social success.
Hammer	– there is something you will need to work hard on.
Heart	– a whole heart is good news for love and romance. A cracked or incomplete heart means that things may not run so smooth...
Hen	– being productive will bring success but take care not to be swindled.

Horse	— a journey will bring benefits.
Horseshoe	— universal symbol of good luck.
Hourglass	— you either need to make a decision quickly or you need to watch over those who are dear to you.
House	— home life will be important.

I

Insect	— problems are minor and will be easily overcome.
Ivy	— a sign of loyalty and loyal friends.

J

Jug	— a symbol of influential friendships and general health and well-being.
Jewelry	— you may expect an increase of wealth or possibly receive a gift.

K

Kangaroo	— unexpected travel.
Kettle	— domestic bliss.
Kite	— wishes will come true.
Knife	— a friendship will be broken.

L

Ladder	— opportunity and the ability to advance yourself.
Lamb	— change and new ideas.
Leaves	— good fortune is coming.
Light bulb	— you will help a friend in need.
Lion	— influential friends will be important.
Lipstick	— you are trying too hard to impress someone, and need to be more natural.
Lock	— obstacles lie in your path.
Loop	— avoid impulsive actions, or you'll end up going around in circles.

M

Man	— a visitor will call on you.
Mermaid	— misfortune! Especially for sailors!
Monkey	— be cautious!
Moon	— changes are on the way.

Mountains	– you will need commitment to reach your goals.
Mouse	– someone will steal an idea or your heart...
Mushroom	– expansion and growth.

N

Nail	– injustice and unfairness lie in your path.
Necklace	– a complete necklace means admirers, a broken one means you may lose the love of one close to you.
Needle	– recognition and admiration will be yours.

O

| Owl | – be cautious, this is a sinister omen. Indicates trouble and loss in business unless caution is taken. |
| Ox | – prosperity; a symbol of friends in high places. |

P

Parasol	– a new lover will come into your life.
Parrot	– someone will be emigrating.
Peanuts	– ignore people who are trying to put you down.
Peacock	– wealth and luxury or a wealthy union.
Pig	– a mixed omen; a faithful lover, but envious friends.
Pipe	– a period of peace and reflection is necessary.
Pyramid	– a secret is about to be revealed that will allow you to move forward.

Q

| Queen | – a queen upon her throne indicates security and stability. Sometimes this can signify attainment to a high position through powerful friends. |
| Question mark | – be cautious. |

R

Rabbit	– growth and new ideas.
Rainbow	– a sign of hope.
Rat	– be cautious; a sign of losses through enemies.
Raven	– a sign of gloom and problems.
Ring	– a marriage! This can also symbolise goodwill and friendship or the completion of a project.

S

Saddle	– you will soon need to go on a journey.
Saw	– hard work.
Scissors	– quarrels and separation.
Sheep	– good fortune will come your way.
Shell	– good news.
Ship	– a worthwhile journey.
Shoe	– a change for the better.
Snake	– spiteful enemies are hiding in wait for you.
Spider	– money is coming your way.
Square	– there are or will be difficulties to overcome.
Squirrel	– you work hard but need to prioritise.
Star	– health and happiness are around the corner.
Steps	– success! You will soon be celebrating.
Sun	– happiness, success and power will be yours.
Sword	– arguments will divide friends.

T

Table	– a reunion.
Teapot	– consultations and meetings.
Telephone	– you will receive an important call soon.
Tree	– health and family will be important.
Triangle	– help will arrive from an unexpected source.

U

Umbrella	– annoyance and trouble.

V

Vase	– a sign of you serving others.
Violin	– a sign of an independent or studious person.
Volcano	– harmful problems are brewing.
Vulture	– a symbol of oppression, cruelty or even theft.

W

Waves	– emotions are running high at this point in time.
Web	– take the advice of those close to you otherwise you could be tangled up in a difficult situation.
Windmill	– grandiose plans will bring rewards.
Wings	– messages are on their way to you.

Witch	– wisdom.
Worms	– secretly something is undermining you.

Y

Yacht	– a sign of increased wealth or happiness.
Yew Tree	– a legacy from an aged relative or friend may come your way.
Yoke	– a position of service.

Z

Zebra	– either you are sought after as a friend or something you have been waiting for will come to fruition.

Tea divination is no easy task, especially for amateurs. Whilst an experienced reader can derive a wealth of meaning from different shapes formed by tea-leaves at the bottom of a cup, a beginner may struggle to distinguish a worm from a snake, which perhaps explains the popularity of novelty fortune telling cups well into the twentieth century.

Tea, fortune telling and the supernatural seem to be intrinsically linked. Annie Horniman had a huge influence on British theatre and is perhaps best known for nurturing the ambitions of performing artists regardless of their income or social standing, aided by a family fortune derived from the sales of Horniman's prepackaged tea. However, aside from her services to British theatre, Annie was a great believer in divination and used tarot cards for guidance in all of her business decisions.

Furthermore, Annie also believed that she could astrally project herself. Horniman and her astral projection associate, Frederick Leigh Gardner, kept very detailed notes about all the planets they visited through astral projection, recording everything from what kind of atmosphere they encountered to some of the conversations they had with the life-forms they met. The diaries certainly make for interesting reading with a strong cup of tea.

The superstitions of tea are not just confined to the leaves left in the bottom of the cup. In some northern parts of England it was believed that a new housewife would not enjoy good luck until she had brewed tea in a teapot of her own in her new home.

In the West Country it was considered a bad omen to pour boiling water into the teapot before the leaves had been added. In the south of England, leaving the teapot lid off signified that a stranger would call on you. It was only asking for trouble if one woman was to pour tea from another woman's pot, as she was leaving herself open to danger.

Tea is the drink that has tided us over in times of need, reviving and restoring us during periods of trouble. The ritual of tea-making and its quirky superstitions have become as ingrained in our culture as the drinking of tea itself.

The history of tea has many dark twists and associations, but it still has a place in the British cup and there is no point crying over spilled leaves. Incidentally spilling leaves is considered good luck in Somerset.

FORTUNES IN TEACUPS, RUBBISH!
YOU KNOW THEY NEVER
COME TRUE,
BUT HERE'S SOME
GOOD LUCK IN ONE,
SO I'M SENDING IT TO YOU!

A postcard from the 1930s.

Bibliography

Alatas, S., *The Myth of the Lazy Native* (London, 1977).

Antrobus, H.A., *A History of Assam Company*, (T&A Constable, Edinburgh, 1957).

Arnold, D. 2004. 'Race, Place and Bodily Difference in Early Nineteenth Century India', Historical Research, May, pp. 254–73.

Barker, G., *A Tea Planter's Life in Assam* (Thacker, Spink & Co, 1884).

Berg, M., *Luxury and Pleasure in Eighteenth-Century Britain* (OUP, 2005).

Berg, M., *The Age of Manufactures 1700-1820: Industry, Innovation and Work in Britain*, 2nd ed (Routledge, New York, 1994).

Bramah, E., *Tea and Coffee: A Modern View of Three Hundred Years Tradition* (Hutchinson of London, 1972).

British Parliamentary Papers, 1837, 'Report from the Select Committee on Aborigines (British Settlements), Vol. 425', Paper 7; 1839, 'The Tea of Assam. Vol. XXXIX', Paper 63; 'Papers Relating to Measures for Introducing Cultivation of Tea Plant in British Possessions in India, Vol. XXXIX', Paper 63; 'Report on the Tea Plant of Upper Assam. India Revenue Consultations, 20 June, 1836. Vol. XXXIX, Paper 63.

Bruce, J., 'Annals of the East India Company: From Their Establishment by the Charter of Queen Elizabeth, 1600, to the Union of the London and English East India Companies, 1707-8'. Vol. III (Black, Perry, and Kingsbury, London, 1810).

Bruce, C.A., 'Report on the Manufacture of Tea, and on the Extend and Produce of the Tea Plantations in Assam', (Adam & Charles Black, Edinburgh, 1839).

Burford, E.J., *Bawds and Lodgings: A History of the London Bankside Brothels* (Peter Owen Publishers, 1976).

Burford, E.J., *London, the Synfulle Citie* (Robert Hale Ltd., 1990).

Campbell, G., *Travels and Adventures in the Province of Assam* (London, 1865).

Chang, Hsin-pao, *Commissioner Lin and the Opium War* (Harvard University Press, 1964).

Charter Granted by Queen Elizabeth to the East India Company, 31 December 1600.

Chesney, K., *The Victorian Underworld*, (Purnell Books Services Ltd. / Maurice Temple Smith Ltd., 1970).

Chesterton, C., *In Darkest London.*

Chinese Repository, (Canton, 1832-1849).

Colley, L., *Britons: Forging the nation 1707-1837*, (Yale University Press, 2009).

Davidson, James W. et al, *Nation of Nations: A Concise Narrative of the American Republic, Vol. 1: to 1877*, 4th ed (McGraw-Hill, New York, 2006).

Dowell, S., *A History of Taxation and Taxes in England from the Earliest Times to the Year, 1885, Vol. 3* (Longmans, Green & Co., London, 1888).

Fortune, R., 'Two Visits to the Tea Countries of China and the British Tea Plantations in the Himalaya; with a Narrative of Adventures, and a Full Description of the Culture of the Tea Plant, the Agriculture, Horticulture, and Botany of China, Vol. 2' (John Murray, London, 1853).

Gelber, Harry G., *Opium, Soldiers and Evangelicals: Britain's 1840-42 War with China, and its Afermath* (Palgrave MacMillan, New York, 2004).

Gurney, J., *Trial of J. Powell.*

Hanes III, W. Travis and Sanello, F. *Opium Wars: The Addiction of One Empire and the Corruption of Another* (Naperville, Il: Sourcebooks, Inc., 2002).

Hansard's Parliamentary Debates, Vols. 39-55, indexed 1838-1840, Vol. 43, April 1840.

Hanway, J., 'An Essay on Tea, Vol. 2', (H. Woodfall, London, 1756).

Harler, C. R. *The Culture and Manufacturing of Tea,* 2nd ed (OUP, 1956).

Hay, D., et al, *Albion's Fatal Tree: Crime and Society in Eighteenth Century England* (Pantheon Books, New York, 1975).

Ibbetson, A., *Tea from Grower to Consumer* 3rd ed (Sir Isaac Pitman & Sons, Ltd, London, 1933)

Inglis, Brian, *The Opium War* (Hodder and Stoughton, 1976).

King, C.W., House of Commons debate on the War with China, 'The Opium Crisis. A Letter to Charles Elliot, Esq. By an American Merchant in Canton'.

The London Pleasure Gardens of the Eighteenth Century. London: Macmillan and Co., Ltd., 1896.

Seer, A. H., *Tea-Cup Reading and the Art of Fortune Telling By Tea Leaves*.

Sharma, J., '"Lazy" Natives, Coolie Labour, and the Assam Tea Industry' (Cambridge University Press, 2008).

Stobart, J., *Sugar and Spice: Grocers and Groceries in Provincial England, 1650-1830* (OUP, 2012).

The Times, 'China. The following are the penalties for buying and smoking opium', Thursday, 4 Oct, 1838, p 8; Issue 16851. *The Times*, 25 December, 1841.

Thelwall, Rev. A.S., M.A., of Trinity College, Cambridge, 'The Iniquities of the Opium Trade with China, &c.' London, 1839.

Thucker, R.C. (ed), *The Marx-Engels Reader*, 2nd ed (W.W. Norton & Company, New York, 1978).

Tinker, H., 'A New System of Slavery: The Export of Indian Labour Overseas, 1830-1920', (London, 1974).

Ukers, W.H., 'All About Tea' Vol. 1 (The Tea and Coffee Trade Journal Company, New York, 1935).

Warren, W.K., *Tea Tales of Assam* (Hampshire, London, 1975).

Wong, J.W.. *Deadly Dreams: Opium, Imperialism, and the Arrow War* (1856-1860) in China.

Xu Naiji, 'Memorial to the emperor for the legalization of opium', in Chinese Repository Vol. 5 (tr Morrision, J.R.) (Cambridge University Press, 1998).

Endnotes

1. Jonas Hanway, pp145-147.
2. Ukers, p39.
3. British Parliamentary Papers, 1837, p76
4. Bruce, R., p.14
5. Ramsay, G.C., 'The Factors which Determine the Varying Degrees of Malarial Incidence in Assam Tea Estates and the Fundamental Principles Governing Mosquito Control of Malaria in Assam', in *Transactions of the Royal Society of Tropical Medicine*
6. See Report of the Assam Labour Enquiry Committee, 1906.
7. Emigration 'A' File No 2-9, February 1889, WAI.
8. This rumour was narrated in 'Proceedings of Assam Labour Enquiry Committee in the Recruiting and Labour Districts', Calcutta, 1906, p58.
9. Prafulladatta Goswami Bihu, *Songs from Assam* (Guwahati) 1988, p20.
10. Revenue A, Nos 77-117, August 1904 (NAI).

Index